There Were Days Like That

Books by Harold P. Levy
A Study in Public Relations
Building a Popular Movement
Public Relations for Social Agencies
There Were Days Like That

There Were Days Like That

by Harold P. Levy

Blue Whale Press
Glendale, California

Restoration of old photographs by Long Photography, Inc.

To Alice
And the Loving Memory
of Phan and Fannie Levy

Contents

*T*his book could not have happened, nor could my two careers and all the memorable events surrounding them, had it not been for the kindnesses of many, many people. With truest humility, I have wondered time and again why—and how—at almost every decisive stage of my life they were there to open doors, to direct me along productive paths, to offer encouragement.

Most of them are identified in the text. And while many no longer are here to hear it from me, I wish to express my deep and loving appreciation and thanks for all that they did. I have not forgotten.

You will come to know most of them in the story that follows.

Two who have been so much a part of all the years of my life are mentioned at many stages but never identified by name. They are my parents, Phan H. and Fannie A. Levy, whose brave and challenging outlook on life contributed much in giving their three sons and daughter a head start.

My mother always called my father Phin (not Phan), perhaps because his true name was Phineas and that would have been the way she met him—though in all my days I never knew him to use that name. Of one of his names, however, he was always most particular: Levy. It is pronounced correctly with a short "e" as in "bevy" or "heavy," and he never failed to correct anyone who ventured to pronounce it otherwise. He also had a never-relaxed rule: he always addressed even his closest friends as Mr. or Mrs. (whatever the last name). He wavered with no one except close relatives. Nor would he permit anyone outside the fold to "first-name" him.

My parents are now gone, too.

I am indebted especially to my wife, Alice, who has been faithful critic, commentator, encourager, and companion throughout the birth of the book and many of the years that preceded it. My warmest thanks go also to our dear friends Louise Howse Macfarlane, a professional librarian and an avid reader and judge of books, whose encouragement has brightened my way from the first page of the manuscript to the last, and Eddie (Mrs. F. Emerson) Andrews, a long-time professional book editor, whose insightful suggestions added immeasurably to the telling of this tale.

Another who contributed greatly is Mrs. Clara C. Dunning, historian and landscape painter of Trinidad, Colorado. We never have met, but it was my good fortune to "find" her through the recommendation of a Trinidad newsman. She was abundantly helpful in researching and providing information about Trinidad in the early years of the 20th century. We have corresponded and spoken by telephone. My thanks to her.

Harold P. Levy

Glendale, California

*M*y parents would tell how they waited until I was of an age to travel to leave Trinidad, Colorado, for Seattle: Trinidad, where they had met and married and where my middle brother and I were born. And how when I was 5 months old, the day came when they boarded the train with their family of three sons, one 5, one nearly 4, the third their infant in arms, bound for their Grand Adventure.

The move had been planned even before my arrival—although the choice of Seattle was more happenstance than otherwise. Both parents were young; my father was 22, my mother 20 when they married in 1900. Both were spirited, and they could anticipate the limitations for their children in a coal town in a remote part of southern Colorado.

Happily, they shared a high degree of independence—notably, in their determination to be free to establish their own way of life detached from elders, siblings and in-laws. Who could have foreseen that within five or six years of our move, elders, siblings and in-laws would begin migrating to "our" city from various parts of the country, including Trinidad, as though drawn by a familial magnet? Unanticipated as the inflow was, I can remember that each new contingent made our home a stopping place until its members had established themselves. For my little sister (who was born in Seattle) and for me, it was generally exciting, with new cousins—some our own ages—aunts and uncles suddenly appearing, although in later years I came to know what a physical hardship it proved for my mother.

While awaiting my birth and travel-worthiness, my parents explored the question: where to move?

The discovery of gold in Alaska in 1897 and the continuing excitement that it generated certainly influenced their thinking in favor of the Northwest. Random thought was given to Alaska, but it was soon dismissed as my father realized it would be no proper life for a

1

wife and three small children. Besides, he well knew that he was no miner, nor was he cut out to be a storekeeper in mining country. His love was the land. He could see himself in the business of real estate, and that was the way it turned out.

To help themselves decide where in the Northwest to head—they had somehow heard of Tacoma—my father and mother talked it over with a trainmaster friend, who had a ready answer. As a railroad man, he knew what they perhaps did not: that Seattle, a little-known lumbering town when Alaskan gold was discovered, had become an important center of commerce, an outfitting point for northbound prospectors and the place to which Alaskan miners shipped their gold . . . that three major railroads were now linked to the city . . . that its population (3,500 in 1880, 42,800 in 1890, 80,671 in 1900) had passed 150,000 and was rising.

So Seattle it became. And as time neared for their August 1907 takeoff, their furniture and other belongings were crated and sent to the railroad station to await the day when proper labels would be attached and everything loaded for the 1,500-mile trip to a new world.

What sort of world were we leaving?

Trinidad in the early 1900s was a self-sufficient little city with a population of less than 10,000 and more or less all the requisites of the times. Among them: 2 commercial banks, 7 hotels, 13 dry goods establishments, 12 barbers, 18 blacksmiths, 7 livery stables, a brewery, 12 general stores, 24 groceries, 22 saloons, 4 laundries (2 of them Chinese) and 5 newspapers.

It had a public library, a foundry, an ice plant, 4 cigar factories and a brick-making plant (some of whose bricks still paved the city's streets into the 1980s), and 10 houses of worship (including the oldest synagogue in Colorado, Temple Aaron). Also a paid fire department, a waterworks, a sewer system, gas and electric lights, 2 telephone and 2 telegraph systems, 4 public schools, a Catholic academy, a business college and a normal school.

And it was served by 3 railroads.

In all of its years, going back to 1876, the date of incorporation and the year Colorado was admitted to the union, Trinidad's population rarely exceeded 13,000. But it was important as the railroad shipping point for coal mined at nearby fields and it was the principal trading center for a wide area.

Situated on the Mountain Branch of the Santa Fe Trail, at the northerly end of Raton Pass, Trinidad early became a resting place and supply center for travelers who made it through the arid plains of eastern Colorado and a watering-feeding stop for stock before the drive over the pass. The Purgatoire River flows through the town.

At times it was also the hangout for such colorful figures as Wyatt Earp, Doc Holiday, Billy the Kid and William Barclay "Bat" Masterson, who was once Trinidad's city marshal.

How Trinidad became the mecca for my mother's family, which migrated from Russia by way of Montreal when she was a tiny girl, I would not know. Unless, as one Trinidad resident and local historian has said, many European immigrants, beset by hard times, were attracted to the area by the well-publicized prosperity of its coal mines.

In any case, my maternal grandparents settled there, raising a family of four sons and three daughters—my mother, the eldest of the girls, being required to assume housekeeping responsibilities for prolonged periods due to my grandmother's often poor health.

Nor do I know what led my father to Trinidad. I do know that he was a free spirit with a sense of adventure. Also born in Russia, on his parents' farm near Kovna, he was dispatched to the United States alone at the age of 16, his father and mother (whom I never saw) wanting to save him from conscription in the Russian army. He left home with a remarkable education; he was studying to be a rabbi, and his command of Hebraic literature and Talmudic learning remained with him throughout his life—as did his facility with languages: Hebrew and Yiddish, German, a variety of Scandinavian tongues, Spanish and, of course, English.

As a young immigrant he did what others from the Old Country did: he became a pack-carrying peddler, traveling mostly through Wisconsin and Minnesota farm country. He told many a tale of being welcomed everywhere as a bringer of both merchandise and news of the outside world, urged to remain overnight at home after home, treated like an honored guest.

Thanks to a lifelong sense of humor, he could relate incidents long years after they happened in which he often was the butt of his own miscalculations—if not folly.

One of these took place in his days as a peddler when he was invited to spend the night with a farm family in rural Minnesota.

Stranger though he was, he was accorded the full hospitality of the house. Dinner was as lavish a farm feast as he had ever enjoyed, and

3

Portraits of my parents, made soon after their marriage on April 8, 1900, in Trinidad.

as it ended he expressed his pleasure and compliments to his hostess, taking note particularly of the succulence of the roast—the most delicious veal, he said, that he had ever tasted.

Visibly pleased, she nevertheless offered one correction.

"That," she told him, "wasn't veal. It was a pork roast."

And with that—to a young man raised in an Orthodox home where pork was forbidden food, and he a once-incipient rabbi to boot—what had been ambrosia suddenly turned to gall. With the resilience of youth, he was able to cover himself but learned that thereafter he must take a careful, rather than carefree, approach to the food placed before him.

Ultimately giving up peddling, he traveled, among other places, to Colorado in pursuit of a new idea: buying and selling horses. Presumably, Trinidad was on his "beat." And romance and marriage held him there, though as a young married couple, my parents lived for a year or two in Salt Lake City, where my elder brother was born, then briefly in La Junta before returning to Trinidad.

And what sort of world did we enter?

What my parents probably neither thought nor cared about was that the year they chose to move was the year of the panic of 1907, which struck in March with virtually no warning. Known as a man-manipulated panic, it was called by the *Commercial and Financial Chronicle,* the period's authority on banking opinion in Wall Street, "the greatest of all panics." Great or not, it was no more than a prelude to what was to strike 23 years later—the Great Depression—with its devastating impact on millions upon millions of lives (many having come through 1907 virtually unscathed) and the inspiration for revolutionary changes in the nation's social, economic and political directions.

Severe as it was elsewhere, the panic seemed to have little effect on Seattle's prosperity and growth. Thanks to the Alaska gold rush, the city had already shaken off such hard blows as the 1893 depression, which sent the lumber and shipping industries into a deep slump and unemployment to nervously high levels, and the great fire of 1889, which completely wiped out its 50-block business section.

Seattle in 1907 was upbeat. Probably an indication of the times, the day after our arrival my father landed a job that provided comfortable security while he and my mother planned an orderly integration into new surroundings. Within less than two years, he established his own real estate business and our family was settled in a home of our own, both in the city's Fremont district.

Seattle was no fairy-tale city. In the early and teen years of the century and even beyond, it spawned various bitter chapters—such as its notorious anti-Chinese riots, damaging confrontational strikes and bloody conflict between conservative/reactionary and radical/progressive factions.

But from our early days there, it had a distinctly cosmopolitan flavor: in its mixture of peoples and cultures; its demonstrated interest in the arts, theater and music (the Seattle Symphony Orchestra was organized in 1903); its various quality shops and restaurants featuring most everything from French, Continental and American cuisines to (naturally) fish and game; its sophisticated food stores and bakeries; and its splendid harbor that looked out on the world.

Another significant fact of those times: The state of Washington early in its history demonstrated a high level of social and political progressivism that percolated up and down, to and from Seattle and the state capital in Olympia. In 1905, for example, the state legislature created a Bureau of Labor and enacted laws providing for wage payment in legal tender rather than company script. Woman suffrage was enacted by the legislature in 1909—and ratified in a popular election—10 years after Washington became a state and 11 years before the Woman Suffrage Amendment to the Constitution became the law of the land.

In 1907, the legislature enacted the direct primary and the 16-hour law for railroad crews; in 1911, initiative, referendum and recall laws and an 8-hour day for women workers, a pure food and drug act and industrial insurance laws. And so it went.

In those early days there were four major English-language daily newspapers, one paper printed in German and three in Japanese. Whether or not a mark of sophistication, the City Directory carried advertisements for four advertising agencies. It had a cable-car system plying its steep hills and a street railway system that linked its 58.56 square miles of land; the rest of the city, 35.91 square miles, was water, made up for the most part of four freshwater lakes wholly within city boundaries. By the end of 1910, it was served by 57 steamship lines and 8 railroad lines. It had a fire department with a chief, 4 assistant chiefs and 350 paid firemen, operating at an annual cost of $410,000; a public library with 130,000 volumes; 61 grade schools, 6 high schools and the University of Washington.

The first distinct memory of my life occurred in the summer of 1909, when I was 2.

I was 2½ and my brother Melvin, 7, when this picture was taken outside the family's first home in Seattle.

It was the day my parents took my two brothers and me to the Alaska-Yukon-Pacific Exposition, held on the new University of Washington campus. It was the most spectacular—and successful—event Seattle had staged to that time.

I was too young to understand it all. But I remember the last minute or two of the streetcar ride as our car crept along at the end of a stream of trolleys converging on the scene and my father called out an open window beside us to a peanut vendor on the curb in an Old Country whimsy he sometimes affected: "Chatziyonkel! Peanuts!" The vendor handed up little red-and-green-striped bags of peanuts and pocketed his money.

The greatest moments of the day came as we walked over the broad lawn and came upon a sight to behold.

There were perhaps 20 short, slight men shuffling round and round in a big circle. Dancing. All were naked except for what I later came to know were breechclouts, and their brown skin and long black hair shone in the bright sun.

"Igorotis," my father said. "From the Philippines."

Neither word had meaning for me. But both instantly locked in my mind, never to fade away.

It was dreamlike reality. And it occurred to me some years later to wonder why I, at age 2, was there at all. It was certainly for one of three reasons: (1) in those days there were no baby sitters; (2) my family, the "pioneers," had no relatives in the city to leave a child with; or the most likely (3) my parents wanted their children to share their adventures. And that was the way it was throughout our growing-up years when, in a sense, my mother, father and their offspring grew up together.

*B*etween 1900 and 1910, Seattle's popula-
tion trebled—from 80,671 to 237,194—a rate of growth nine times
higher than for the nation as a whole.

Some of that growth was attributed by commentators of the time
to the incorporation into the city of adjacent smaller towns. But there
were other reasons, and one was the impact of the Alaska-Yukon-Pacific
Exposition.

It was a time of high enthusiasm, when "anything" Seattle dreamed
of was considered possible. Just as it exploited its splendid harbor to
become a major seaport city, just as it sold itself over other hopeful
cities as *the* logical Northwest terminus for transcontinental railroads,
just as it razed its hills to open the downtown business section to
expansion, this time it succeeded in building the Exposition into a world
event from an off-the-cuff idea broached only four years earlier.

It was no surprise that in one day in 1907 (the year of the panic)
the people of Seattle bought $650,000 worth of Exposition stock to
help move the project along and later added another $150,000, for a
total of $800,000. Nor was it out of character when Exposition trustees
succeeded in gaining sizeable appropriations from the state of Washington, from neighboring states and states farther removed and from
Congress.

The AYP, as the Exposition came to be known, received such favorable publicity around the nation and much of the rest of the world
before and after it opened that it drew a giant attendance of 3,740,000
in its four-and-a-half-month run: June 1 to October 16, 1909. Dig-
nitaries came from far away: statesmen, political leaders, industrialists,
writers. President William Howard Taft was there, along with other
notables from the nation's capital, governors of many states (including
New York Governor Charles Evans Hughes, later to be Chief Justice

of the Supreme Court) and personages from other nations, including ambassadors to the United States Jean Jules Jusserand of France and Baron Takahira of Japan.

In addition to the United States and its relatively new acquisition, Alaska, countries that had exhibits—many in pavilions of their own—included Canada, Great Britain, France, Germany, Russia, the Netherlands, Chile, China, Japan, Columbia, Costa Rica, Ecuador, Nicaragua, Guatemala, Panama, Honduras, El Salvador, Mexico, Peru, India, the Philippines, Dutch East Indies, French East Indies, German Colonies, Formosa, Korea, New Zealand and Siam.

Many visitors who came to see chose to stay.

Staging the Exposition was a bold step for a city that had come into being barely more than a half century earlier under most rudimentary circumstances.

It was in February 1852 when the first white men—a party of four pioneer-settlers newly arrived from the Midwest—set foot on the site. So impressed were they with their find that they promptly staked claims for themselves under the "Donation Law" and, honoring a friendly Indian chief, Sealth, called the place Seattle.

Until then, the sole inhabitants were Indians of the Duwamish and Suquamish tribes, and until then the land had been theirs.

The site was a hilly stretch that rose above a protected deep-water harbor: Elliott Bay, the inner arm of Puget Sound. It was heavily forested and watered by springs and running streams.

The four founding fathers would be remembered as heroes of their time and place, their deeds and the stories of their families recorded in histories of Seattle and the Northwest.

They were Arthur A. Denny; his younger brother, David T. Denny; Carson D. Boren—three members of a party of 15 adults and children who left Illinois in April 1851 to travel the Overland Trail to Oregon by covered wagon—and William N. Bell, another covered-wagon migrant, who with his family joined the Denny-Boren party on the trail. Arthur Denny's granddaughter, Roberta Frye Watt, who grew up with tales of the historic trek, preserved many of them in her 1931 reminiscence, *The Story of Seattle*.

She told how it was pure chance that turned the pioneers' plans around and sent the party, not to their intended destination, but to the place that would become Seattle.

They knew where in the West they were going: they were bound for Oregon's fertile Willamette Valley, where they would settle and become farmers. And that was how it was until they pushed well into Oregon Territory and heard enticing tales of a land that was new to them: the Puget Sound country. What persuaded them beyond question were the accounts by a friendly stranger from Oregon City who happened to be on the trail and happened to camp near them one night— a man who clearly knew the Northwest. What he related was music to their ears: the mild climate, the fertile soil, the magnificent beauty of a region ripe for settlers—a region unlike the Willamette Valley, which was already alive with homesteaders—where land was freely available. Moreover, Puget Sound was roughly as near to them as was Portland at the time, though there was yet no road there through the mountains.

All of which was enough for them.

They drove on to Portland, a town then of more than 800, spent only enough time to organize themselves for their new destination and sailed north in early November, just short of seven months from the day they had departed Illinois in their covered wagons.

The party, now grown to 24 (12 adults, 12 children), booked passage on the little schooner *Exact,* which was ferrying gold prospectors to the Queen Charlotte Islands off the coast of British Columbia. Eight days out of Portland, the *Exact* reached Elliott Bay and anchored well out in the water. The pioneers and their belongings were rowed ashore and the little ship continued north with the gold seekers.

The point of landing was a rolling beach backed by a wooded shoreline. And that was where the pioneers lived their first winter months, beset with rain and meandering Indians whose intentions were not easily determined. They called the place variously Alki (meaning "by-and-by" in Chinook) and with a note of bravado, New York-Alki.

In later years, Alki Beach and the extended area surrounding it would be part of Seattle, and in my childhood the beach was a favorite family picnic ground.

Alki was tolerable as a temporary foothold, but the two Dennys, Boren and Bell had other ideas. They came to know of the heavy demand for Northwest timber in burgeoning San Francisco. Surrounded as they were by rich stands of fir and cedar, they were certain they could participate in the thriving market by not only harvesting the timber but shipping it expeditiously and economically. That called for a deep-water harbor to enable ships to dock, load cargoes, sail away and return from California with supplies—and more pioneers.

11

Studying the scene across the water, they were sure they had it. And they were right. The day came when they took to an Indian canoe, paddled across the bay and found what they were looking for: deep water and abundant forests. They would gladly have foregone the steep, rugged hills rising from the shoreline, for they still had farming on their minds. But all together this was their Promised Land.

Ships came. Trade developed. Newcomers continued to arrive. The settlement prospered and grew into a city. And ultimately the hills would go, demonstrating once again how "anything" seemed possible in the hands of dreamers-become-activists.

The time came near the close of the century when the hills that Arthur Denny and his co-founders wished had not been there began to stifle the growth of the business heart of the city—landlocked, as it was, by natural barriers and confined to a relatively limited area adjacent to the waterfront.

The harbor was immediately to the west of the business district. To the south were tideflats, covered much of the time by tidewater. To the north and east: hills so high that they blocked penetration to the opposite side.

Most massive of all was Denny Hill—named for the two founding Dennys—which rose variously 240 to 300 feet and more. Formidable as it was, it nevertheless had been built up with houses, apartments and hotels, including the city's most elegant of all, the Denny Hotel, at its crest. Getting past it, however, was another matter. No streets existed to facilitate the city's logical expansion north and east.

Finally, agitation for relief brought the first steps toward solution. By 1904, at the urging of most of the affected property owners (whose land values were held down by prevailing conditions), First and Second Avenues were cut through the westerly side of the hill and two east-west streets were similarly regraded for short distances. The work was performed by the traditional resources of the time: manpower, horse-drawn scoops and horse-drawn wagons.

Then came agitation to do away with Denny Hill entirely. It was a project deemed so costly that some property owners demurred, and a compromise was worked out to undertake only the larger segment of the hill, the remainder deferred until later—which turned out to be 1929–30.

What followed was a conception, born about 1906, to sluice away the hills and use the dirt to fill the tideflats. Engineers adapted the idea from sluicing methods used in Alaska mining operations but carried it a few steps further. The essential water was drawn from Lake Union, about a mile and a half distant, and pumped through 24-inch pipe to the top of Denny Hill, and the dirt was conveyed to the bay. Engineers even found a way to expedite the removal of standing structures: turning water on them to undermine them and letting them tumble into holes, where they were set afire.

Thus, downtown was refashioned and some 1,400 acres of tideland bordering Elliott Bay were filled to become sites for commerce and industry. The two Dennys and Bell were gone, but Carson Boren, the fourth founding father, was alive to witness the transformation. He died in 1912.

When regrade operations were completed, it was calculated that 41.5 million cubic yards of dirt had been moved, a volume exceeded only by the amount of dirt dug to build the Panama Canal.

The rebuilding of the inner city—particularly the sluicing away of the hills—was a feat that captured nationwide attention: reported, described and analyzed at length in the press, engineering publications and academic and popular journals.

As a small child, I heard talk among my elders about the Denny Regrade. And how big streams of water were used to wash down the hills. All of this was not very meaningful to me: I could see that the hills were gone, but I could not figure out what a Denny Regrade was.

My memories of downtown Seattle from my early and later childhood are, for the most part, a succession of fragmentary incidents—vignettes—that occasionally left their mark as learning experiences.

One of those learning experiences occurred on a particularly lovely day when I was perhaps 6. My then-favorite cousin, Earle, about my age, and his parents had come from Raton, New Mexico, to pay us a visit. We were strolling along a downtown street: he and I ahead, our parents trailing behind, when he spied a fruit store with a sidewalk display. Rushing over, he picked up a small handful of red cherries. Not to be outdone, I followed suit. But mine was a short-lived triumph, ending with a quick, sharp rebuke from my parents. They commanded me to return the cherries, which I did, and to go up to the storekeeper and apologize, which I did. My embarrassment was almost overwhelming, so much so that only later did I realize that my cousin had received no parental reprimand and had kept his cherries. It was a lesson well learned: my first and last venture into pilfering.

Double exposure—Adorned with a new hair ribbon, a second birthday gift from an adoring aunt, Leah poses soberly outside our home while her forlorn elder brother, the author, housebound with some childhood ailment, steals a peak. It all happened just as our mother clicked her Brownie camera and recorded a picture for posterity.

Although suburban Fremont, where we lived and my father had his business, was a long streetcar ride away, it was downtown where the family's principal shopping took place. I am not sure why my mother often chose me to accompany her on shopping excursions, unless it was that I was not yet in school as my brothers Melvin and Davy were— and they, in any case, would likely have considerd themselves too grown up for such expeditions. My sister Leah was as yet too little.

In those days, Second Avenue was the heart of the business district. First Avenue—the once undisputed business center and scene of the landmark Totem Pole in Pioneer Square—retained its marks of quality. Streets to the east—Third, Fourth, Fifth, Sixth and up the scale of numbered streets—had buildings and businesses, but their day was yet to come. Second Avenue was where all the principal department stores— no less than five—the major specialty shops, shoe stores, clothing stores, jewelry stores, music stores, hotels, office buildings and other enterprises were to be found. At its upper end stood a multistoried building, the Standard Furniture Company, with a huge sign on the roof: "Your Credit is Good." Moving southward, stores and buildings lined both sides of the street; there were no vacant lots. You passed the three cable car lines—Madison Street, James Street and Yesler Way—as they crossed Second Avenue. Beyond were the skid road district, the fringes of Chinatown and, within hailing distance, the two railroad stations.

There was so much to see.

The *Seattle Times* occupied a stone building on the prime corner of Second and Union. You could look in a ground-floor window and see pages of the day's paper on display. Always in the lower right corner of page one was the weather report featuring a cartoon called "Doc's Dippy Duck," with a cartoon weatherman sporting an odd hat resembling a tiny striped umbrella, his cartoon duck beside him.

The principal theaters were on Second Avenue, including the Pantages, the great vaudeville house. I can still remember the candy butchers walking the aisles between acts, their wares in boxlike carriers suspended by straps around their necks. It was there, too, that my mother and I saw a wondrous enactment of the sinking of the *SS Titanic*. The entire stage was given over to miniature ships plying a make-believe ocean. Then the *Titanic* on its maiden voyage. We saw it strike the iceberg and sink before our eyes.

The class motion picture theater of the time, the Clemmer Theater, was on Second Avenue as, I am sure, were others since forgotten.

It was on my first remembered family shopping trip to J. Redel-sheimer & Company—called simply Redelsheimer's—a prominent First Avenue clothing store, that I experienced another marvel of my then 3 or 4 years of age: a moving stairway that traveled between the first and second floors. If it was called an escalator, I have no memory of that.

Another First Avenue store that made a lasting impression was Augustine & Kyer, a specialty grocery where the clerks wore long white aprons and the selection of meats (including game birds in full feather), vegetables, fruits and other food seemed both bountiful and beautiful.

I retain repeated memories of Indian women—squaws—from reservations across Puget Sound who always sat or squatted on the sidewalk in front of Rhodes Department Store—always Rhodes, never nearby Bon Marche or Frederick & Nelson down the street—presiding over displays of hand-woven basketry spread out on blankets, an occasional customer pausing to inspect and buy.

And of a disturbing sight we saw one day as we looked down one of the steep cobblestone streets between Second and First. A drayman seated in his wagon was driving downhill when one of his team of horses slipped and fell in his traces. Unable to get up, his legs pinned beneath him, the horse slid the length of the hill while the driver whipped him relentlessly. I have wondered over the years whether the driver expected to beat the poor beast to his feet or whether, perhaps, he may have been overcome with embarrassment at being the center of such a scene and reacted with unreasoned anger.

Many happy times were associated with downtown. One was our Saturday family outings, when the six of us would attend one—and sometimes two—movies, then pay a visit to an elegant ice cream parlor where luscious sundaes were set before us.

As I grew older, I often accompanied my father, a consummate food shopper, on trips to the Pike Place Farmers Market. It was a living cornucopia of fresh vegetables and fruits harvested each morning by farmers who hauled them in, then presided over their wares from their own stalls. The market was given over in part to cut-rate grocery stores, meat markets, fresh-fish stands and open fruit stands selling produce from elsewhere, such as oranges, bananas and small crates of tangerines imported from Japan—commonly known as "Jap oranges." The spirited rivalry among the farmers and merchants as they hawked their wares to passing customers gave it all a circus atmosphere.

Whether consciously or not, my father was passing his shopping expertise along to me, and it proved one never-forgotten fact of my early training.

Memorable as downtown experiences were, it was those closer to home that are remembered as the sweetest, perhaps because that was where the growing up really occurred—where the very young years were a continuing succession of adventures—though at the time there was no good way to appreciate that.

What would happen happened, that is all. Sometimes it left happy feelings; sometimes it hurt. Other times were little more than fleeting incidents that gave neither pleasure nor pain.

That is the way it was with me, and it may be the way it is with everyone. Only when you have accumulated enough experience to be able to evaluate one distinct moment in life against another do you retroactively appraise the quality of fragmentary early adventures.

In those days, suburban Fremont was linked to downtown Seattle, as well as to much of the rest of the city, by Westlake Avenue, a long, wandering street that skirted the west shore of Lake Union and offered views of the entire lake and the residential areas on the hills above it to the east. This was the route of the Fremont streetcar line, the interurban rail line between Seattle and Everett and of street traffic, both motorized and horse drawn.

Entering and leaving Fremont, you crossed a grade-level wooden bridge over a narrow waterway that later would become part of the Lake Washington Ship Canal; the canal, completed in 1916, that connected Puget Sound with Lake Union and its near neighbor, Lake Washington, affording deep-water ships access to the freshwater harbor inside the city. The canal would also mark the end of the wooden bridge, which gave way to a steel drawbridge, which in turn would be replaced by the high-level, fast-speed Aurora Bridge, bypassing old Fremont— but that bridge came after my days in Seattle.

It was the wooden bridge—or the water flowing beneath it—that afforded me a once-in-a-lifetime experience: watching an Indian spear salmon making their way from Puget Sound to Lake Union. I knew he was an Indian, not by his dress, which was much like any other rough-and-ready attire, but because I was told so and was told, too, that Indians, unlike their white neighbors, had the privilege of fishing in that manner whenever they chose.

No matter where we had been, once we crossed the wooden bridge to Fremont, it felt like home, even if "home" was literally still miles away.

You came first to Fremont's business district, covering several square blocks; this was where my father's office was. Leading eastbound from the business district was the closest thing we then had to a boulevard. It was a wide street along the northerly side of the lake, past two or three sawmills on the lake shore, where you breathed the good smell of newly sawn lumber, past small shipyards and on to neighboring communities much like our own: Wallingford, and then the University District, seat of the University of Washington.

Two other principal landmarks from which my growing-up experiences radiated were the B. F. Day public school, the grade school we all attended, and our third home in Fremont, on Sunset Place (uninspiringly renamed Francis Avenue, again after my time in Seattle). This third home was only five blocks from Woodland Park and something less than two miles from school.

One cherished memory was a game my sister Leah and I played as we walked to school on gloriously fresh spring mornings in late May and early June. The lawns we passed were Northwest green. The lilacs, sweet peas, nasturtiums, roses—all spring flowers—were blooming. Robins, house wrens, song sparrows—all summertime visitors—were back and in full voice.

School always closed for the summer by mid-June. But the time would come when it seemed impossible to wait any longer for vacation.

So we played what we called "Let's talk vacation."

In our early days, the talk was mostly variations on remembered summertime fun. We would recapture how we would soon be going on picnics and into the water at Alki Beach, joined by one or two other families with children we knew. We would talk of picnics our mother would take us on to Woodland Park and how *this time* I would really capture a crow with my hatchet. And how our mother (to us she was "Mama," just as our father was "Papa") would prepare picnic lunches for the two of us to eat under the big yellow-transparent apple tree on the lawn beside our house. And how we would gather hazelnuts that grew profusely—and wild—on vacant lots near home. And how we would surely go on weekend, or longer, family camping trips. And how we would surely spend a week or two in a cottage at Richmond Beach, my mother shepherding her younger children during the day and my father and elder brother joining us after work.

The family's third home, on Sunset Place, in Seattle. Leah, foreground, was about 5. It was in a small orchard at the rear where I bagged a luckless English sparrow with my new BB gun and vowed never to kill again.

Leah and the author. Picture was shot outside the family's Sunset Place home in Seattle by an itinerant photographer traveling with goat and cart props.

Except on hard-raining days we walked to and from school; light rain never bothered us. When we rode, it was by streetcar, and like all school children paid our way with tokens priced at 2½ cents, half the adult fare.

One bright morning when, for some reason, I was walking it alone, Frank Ham, a classmate and chum, came riding his bicycle down Fremont Avenue and offered me a lift to school. Of course, I accepted.

This trip taught me one important lesson—*never interfere with the driver.*

Seated on the bar in front of him as we raced downhill gaining speed, I felt my eyes start to water in the wind and a shaky, uncontrollable urge overcame me to "help" him. I put a hand on the handlebar with a little too much thrust, and down we went: Frank, I and the bicycle skidding along the brick pavement. I do not remember that he took me to task; it was barely possible that he didn't realize how much I was to blame. Our friendship survived. But I can't remember that he ever again offered me a ride.

As we occasionally did, my brothers and I went one evening to the Fremont Theater, a simple little movie house a few blocks from home. In those days, the price of admission was a dime. I had seen enough movies to know that I, at age 5 or 6, had a crush on the beautiful actress Anita Stewart. And that night she was the star in a film called, I think, *The Juggernaut*. In any case, the climax came as the train on which she was a passenger started across a trestle high above a deep canyon. As the action had it, the villain got there before the train and somehow damaged the trestle so that it and all the passenger cars came tumbling down. What occupied our conversation on the way home was how clearly nervous and lip-biting the camera showed lovely Anita to be moments before the crash.

My brothers—Melvin, who was to become a novelist, playwright and screen writer, and David (always called Davy), who would be a career motion picture producer—had yet to reach their ultimate level of sophistication. Together, they explained to me that it was because, as an actress, she knew what the script had in store for her—and anyone would be nervous anticipating a violent train wreck.

I was about 7 when I received a BB gun as a gift. I had never before had such a weapon but decided that the best way to learn to handle it was to use it. The big yard behind our house, replete with cherry, quince and assorted other trees, made an ideal training ground. So gun in hand I went out looking for a proper target, and there it

21

No matter how old—or how young—they might be, Melvin and Davy always were, to me, "my big brothers." In this early snapshot, Melvin, left, and Davy.

was: an English sparrow in a tree. Knowing perfectly well that it would take more skill than I then had to down a bird, I took aim, fired—and the poor bird fell, mortally wounded. It was a traumatic experience. I tried to explain it to myself and—seeking solace—telephoned my brother Melvin at work. He was uncertain whether to congratulate or commiserate. Shaken, I gave the bird a decent backyard burial.

From that time on, I lost all interest in firing at any living thing.

Then there was the day my father drove home in an automobile— *our* automobile: the first on the block. We were full of admiration, delight and sheer excitement. I am sure all of us thought it beautiful. But it was a great hulk of a machine, a four-year-old secondhand 1910 Everett touring car. The top fastened to the front fenders with brass rods; brass trim was everywhere. The headlights ran on fuel kept in a tank on the running board; come dusk, my father had to hand-light them—just as he had to get out and crank every time the engine died.

We took trips in that car—drives as long as 25 miles (each way) to Auburn, where my grandparents then lived. Breakdowns became an expected part of these trips. Generally, it was stripped gears. Until my parents decided that we'd had enough of our old Everett and got rid of it. By 1916, we had our first new car, an Overland. It was the name, I am sure, that won my father's heart. No other car would do—not even a Studebaker, once under consideration as the next new car and much admired by the rest of the family. But it was always Overlands.

Another time, I went out to play only to hear the clanging of a fire engine in the near distance. Following the sound, I tracked it to a house on a street two or three blocks away, and surely enough the house was in flames.

But there was even more. The engine had come up the long Fremont Avenue hill, over unpaved streets, to the scene of the fire. And there, one of the two horses dropped in his traces—dead. The run was too much for it. (It was not until 1926 that the Fire Department retired the last of its horses and horse-drawn equipment to become completely motorized.) While I and others watched the blaze and the counter-attraction, the firemen remained on their job until the fire was in hand.

About that time, my mother, fairly frantic over my long absence, arrived on the scene. Not waiting to witness the end of the story, she hustled me home and in motherly fashion, including a lick or two on my bottom, advised me to "never let it happen again."

Then there was the time I was out playing marbles with a new boy on the block. He was far more skillful than I, and I wondered if the word he addressed to his taw whenever he had a particularly difficult shot had anything to do with it. It was a word I had never heard before.

That evening as the family awaited dinner—which we always celebrated together—I was on the dining room floor engrossed in the funnies. Not atypically, Davy started teasing me until, patience exhausted, I let fire with my new word: "Leave me alone, you cocksucker." And that was the last word.

My father grabbed me off the floor, rushed me to an upstairs room, invited me to drop my trousers, gave me the spanking of my life and told me I was missing dinner that night.

This was another lesson learned—*never use words you don't understand.*

My father didn't explain the word, and it was long years before I had any inkling as to what it meant. I often wonder whether my father did all the right things that evening. But there was no question: I learned!

*I*n 1919, when I was 12, I began to recognize that the world as I had known it was giving way to another. This expressed itself in varied ways. It was the year we left Fremont and moved to a larger home on Capital Hill, a more affluent part of the city. My father had moved his office downtown. My brothers, now attending the University of Washington (though still living at home), had new interests and associations—new lives of their own—and the close family relationship of earlier years was loosening. My sister and I had changed schools and were now enrolled at Stevens, a somewhat smaller school than B. F. Day, where she would complete the seventh and eighth grades and I the eighth.

And I was nearing a fateful decision—the choice of a career, made without parental direction or influence, and never to be regretted.

Probably nothing escapes change with the passing of time: people and cities alike. Seattle was experiencing a growing maturity of its own—even to being able to boast the tallest building west of Chicago, the L. C. Smith Tower, built in 1914, rising 42 stories above Second Avenue.

With the coming of World War I, the city began to change at a breathtaking pace.

As always, the rise and fall of two of Seattle's key industries, lumber and shipbuilding, affected its level of prosperity, and the wartime industrial boom took it to a record peak. Twenty shipyards, running at full capacity and employing 40,000, built more ships than any other port in the nation. The airplane industry (long nurtured, if not born, in Seattle) was in high gear as government orders poured in for planes. Those same government orders sent lumber prices soaring. Lumber mills operated at their highest levels, and mill workers poured into the city to fill an abundance of jobs.

Overall prosperity cast a euphoric spell over the city. But it lasted only a short time.

When the war ended in 1918, the lumber market collapsed. Prices began to fall. Trade declined. And with the closing down of war industries, unemployment rose and wages dropped.

Affected by the post-war unrest, shipyard workers struck, and an open-shop campaign began in the ranks of employers who hoped to weaken the unions.

All this brought on a general strike, generating fears that worsened with the recognition that this was the first such strike in the United States and might spread throughout the nation. More than 75,000 walked out on February 6, 1919, and succeeded in crippling much of the city's business life—stores, newspapers, plants, mills, restaurants, barber shops, public transportation and more. Even the schools were closed.

The strike lasted only five days and ended peaceably. But it gained immediate national attention as "the Seattle Revolution" and national acclaim for Mayor Ole Hanson, who spent $50,000 of public money to enlist special police and deputize 2,400 businessmen and received credit—even on the front page of the *New York Times*—for ending the "revolution." The strike committee itself had organized labor guards to preserve order and maintain vital services. But Mayor Hanson had his moment as voices throughout the country sang his praise and a spontaneous mini-campaign started, boosting him for President.

That, too, died. But I remember my father as one of those who considered the presidential "campaign" a joke. He knew Hanson as a fellow realtor who had entered and won the mayoral race but never demonstrated qualifications anywhere near those of the presidency. Hanson returned to real estate and won attention in that field as the promoter who put San Clemente, an oceanfront community south of Los Angeles, on the map.

For my part, I remember the strike as the genesis of the jitney bus. With public transportation halted, anyone with an automobile was permitted to post a jitney sign on his car and haul passengers at the regular streetcar fare of 5 cents (a "jitney") or whatever more the rider was willing to pay.

A wave of repressive action followed the general strike, with raids and arrests directed against unionists, socialists and Industrial Workers of the World (IWWs) amid fears of "the bolshevik menace." It was ironic that Seattle and the Northwest, a region historically progressive,

erupted periodically into confrontations—sometimes bloody, sometimes deadly—between interests opposed to organized labor and others
supporting it and interests opposed to one minority or another and the
victims of their wrath.

Unlike adventures experienced in very young years, one early teen-
age discovery is that you are truly in a new world. Your adventures no
longer simply happen. Now they are largely self-generated.

The bicycle that came into my life when I was 12 or 13 provided
living proof of the discovery.

Not too many months after our move to the new home, my parents
agreed the time had come for me to have a bicycle. The three of us
agreed further that it was only reasonable for me to pay off the $30 or
$35 investment at a rate, as I remember, of $1 a month, earned or saved
from very limited spending money. And that I did. (Later, the first job
I found for myself, as a summer-vacation page at the Seattle Public
Library, paid 25 cents an hour, and that also contributed to paying off
the investment.)

The bicycle meant new freedom.

I never rode it to school, but it enabled me to explore areas miles
from home and I rode it willingly on errands. It took me and a bicycle-
owning pal on a few weekend camping trips—gear tied to handlebars—
mostly to a wooded area with a running stream, perhaps 15 miles south
of the city limits: a place called Des Moines. And it took me to the
home (that is, outside the home) of a girl I knew from Sunday school—
the most beautiful girl I thought I had ever seen. She had lovely black
hair and a medium-olive complexion and her name was Rebecca. I was
too timid ever to tell her how I thought of her. And too timid ever to
get off my bike, go to the door and ask for her. So time after time I
spent long minutes at the curb hoping she would come out-of-doors
so I could say how fortunate it was that I was just passing by. But she
never did and I never did.

A year melted away; then came high school. (The intermediate-
level junior high had not yet entered the Seattle school system.)

Unexpected good fortune made my entry into life as a high schooler
feel as though it were arranged by benign gods. Because of the location
of our new home, I was one of about 300 "saved" from having to
enroll in one or another of the city's older high schools (mine would
have been old, old Broadway High). I became part of the freshman
class in brand-new East High—so new that, hastily built, it was simply

a sprawling portable-type wooden building; a year later it gave way to a modern two-story structure, on the same spread of land, named, or renamed, Garfield High.

Mine was a class of pioneers who had a voice in making the rules, naming our sports teams (the Bulldogs), the school newspaper (the *Messenger*), and the annual (the *Arrow*) and choosing the school colors (purple and white).

In those days I had begun what could generously be called creative writing, turning out short stories that received, at best, casual response from the few I trusted to read them. There were also essay-type sketches of one kind or another and poems, one of which was published in an obscure journal. I received no payment but felt deeply rewarded because my name was attached to it.

Surely, my inclination was in the direction of writing.

So I was ripe for what happened in the first days of my high school journalism class. It was presided over by a good-humored young teacher named Harry Post, who told us that it would be our responsibility to do most of the writing and editing for the school paper. All together, it was a happy experience for me and pointed so clearly in one direction that I told myself with total conviction that this, journalism, was to be my career. More than anything else, I determined to become a news-paperman. And that was the way it turned out.

Only one personal matter remained to be resolved: What about my music? From the time I was about 6 I had taken piano lessons, passing through the hands of two teachers until the third, Adam Jardine, entered my life—or I his. He was a superbly gentle, instructive teacher who led me to realize that practice was not a chore but a creative pleasure. He also taught me that any upcoming pianist should be versed in the newer dissonant music as well as the works of the romantic composers. He became increasingly pleased with my command of the piano and dropped repeated suggestions that I consider music—the piano—as my career.

Although I continued to study with him through high school and most of my university days, I gradually found the pressures on my time increasing and the opportunity to practice lessening. Working my way through school, as I did, and recognizing that nothing would break my commitment to newspapering, I parted sadly from Mr. Jardine. Thereafter, the piano as a serious consideration faded more and more from my life.

As in any young life, high school years yielded good times and less good times and memories of greater and lesser significance.

To conserve space, in our freshman year classrooms were small and two rows of desks were paired side by side, with narrow aisles separating them from the next two rows. There was a day in our English class when my near neighbor Bill Lane poked me and whispered his new discovery.

"Look," said Bill, "if you cross your fingers and touch your nose it feels like you have two noses." I did, found he was right and broke out laughing. Our teacher, Miss Walters, unaware of what had gone on before, saw nothing funny in my laughter and invited me to leave the room. Meanwhile, the discoverer of the two-nose theory remained benignly silent and experienced no problems.

A day or two later, Miss Walters and I had an amiable reconciliation, but I believe she never did learn how to experience the sensation of two noses.

An all-city high school Shakespeare contest was announced one year, with preliminary runoffs for contestants in each school. I determined to enter and also to bypass the opportunity to enlist the help of a teacher as coach, dreaming of bringing down the house with a surprise performance on the day we contestants were to perform before our peers at a school assembly.

My brother Melvin consulted one of his university professors, who suggested the opening lines of King Richard III for a surefire presentation. Carefully memorizing the lines, I worked out pauses, gestures and appropriate moves on stage and felt eminently prepared as the appointed day arrived. When my name was called, I rose in the assembly—by now feeling trembly—strode to the stage with a developing case of stage fright and, forgetting pauses, gestures and moves, rushed into Richard's stirring soliloquy—lines that would be remembered through adulthood:

> Now is the winter of our discontent
> Made glorious summer by this sun of York;
> And all the clouds that lour'd upon our house
> In the deep bosom of the ocean buried.

. . . and on with increasing speed to the end of Richard's speech.

Needless to say, I advanced no further in the contest—and barely heard the friendly ripple of applause as I left the stage and the assembly hall.

You live down such gaffes.

Sometime into high school years, I embarked on the first of two brief entrepreneurial ventures.

As one Christmas season approached I decided to go into the Christmas tree business. The idea: I would solicit orders house-to-house in our Capital Hill community; then when the time came to deliver the trees I would have my father drive out of town with me. We would chop down trees in nearby forests and bring them back in the family car.

Taking orders was no problem. I set prices that seemed right for the times: 50 cents for small trees, 75 cents for large. By the time I had signed up 25 households, I figured that was as many trees as my father and I could haul into town and stopped order-taking.

The impracticality of my tree-harvest idea was brought home to me in a chat with my father.

Having orders and no trees, a brighter idea crossed my mind and I was able to sell it to a corner-lot Christmas tree vendor. He would deliver trees from his stock and we would split the take. So the two of us set out on our rounds one day—and as it turned out, every household but one honored their orders. The vendor and I settled accounts and parted happily.

The second venture was more in keeping with my newly embraced career. I determined to establish a free-distribution weekly newspaper in our Capital Hill community—where no such publication existed—and was well under way before agreeing to admit two partners: high school journalism cronies Norman Reynolds and Mark Sullivan.

We came to terms easily on what seemed a fair distribution of responsibilities. It would be up to me to choose the name of the paper—which turned out to be the *Capital Cub*—and I would serve as editor, principal writer, advertising solicitor and general manager. Reynolds would be a reporter-writer. Sullivan would be general consultant. The two of them would assume financial responsibility for costs not covered by advertising. Profits would be shared equally.

At the time, I saw nothing out of the ordinary in closing a deal with a small downtown printing shop to set type and print 1,500 eight-page copies a week for a grand total of $35 per issue (and the privilege of looking forward to continuing printing business). Nor did I give a second thought to the fact that the trusting proprietor would close the deal with a teenage "publisher" without requiring advance payment.

All three partners were pleased with Issue No. 1, which we hand-delivered to our constituency. My pleasure was increased by at last having one of my short stories in print. Advertising revenue amounted to about $20, which left my partners to share in paying the remaining $15 indebtedness.

Our printing bill paid, we three partners held a post-publication conference and concluded that attending school, publishing a newspaper and covering the loss margin—all at the same time—could prove a heavy burden. Besides, my parents were feeling less than enchanted at having our home function as publication headquarters and having our home telephone burdened with calls from inquiring and contributing readers and would-be advertisers.

So we hailed the first and last issue of the *Capital Cub* and closed out the venture.

It was about that time, too, that my father enlisted my services as an after-school and summertime aide in his real estate business, a relationship that continued throughout my university years.

Had it not been for that father-son business association, I surely would have followed along my brothers' path and found part-time employment elsewhere to help work my way through school—particularly through the university—as both of them did.

The relationship, which extended over a period of some eight years, gave me practical insights into the real estate business. My father's splendid knowledge of real estate and near-brilliant ability to put together profitable deals that pleased all parties provided a learning experience. I not only learned but was able to acquire property of my own which, sadly, would be lost in the coming Depression.

Sad/Happy Days Remembered

By the time I reached my teen years it was clear that my father's often-expressed wish—never to be a rich man—was sure to be fulfilled. It is only right to say, however, that his negative view toward wealth, which he feared would bridle a man's free spirit, was more than balanced by his determination to provide well for his family—a determination sometimes frustrated.

We lived through good times and bad: times of financial well-being and others nervously precarious. They seemed to occur intermittently and alternately.

How much his aversion to accumulating wealth had to do with the ups and downs was hard to tell. Other self-imposed guidelines and outside forces played their part. For instance, my father would never sue in the courts, no matter how "right" his cause and no matter that he had personal friends—judges, attorneys, bankers, political figures—in significant places. Nor would he ever have a partner in business, even to balance his consummate skill as a real estate practitioner with others' greater talent in business management—as he had opportunities to do. And then, of course, there was Seattle's up-and-down economy with its up-and-down effects on the real estate market.

The good times were euphoric. All the way from palmy days when we acquired our first automobile, then succeeding cars . . . when our living standard rose with newly purchased homes . . . when my father indulged in extravagant gifts for my mother—jewelry and others—and surprise gifts for the children . . . when the two of them would shop for new furnishings, silverware and other appointments for the home and for *our* rooms . . . when they would stock abundant larders, even to boxes of apples and oranges, stored in the basement, which we were welcome to draw on as we liked as treats for our playmates.

Then there were times when the larder was lean and retrenchment was the way of life.

We never went hungry. But there were periods when my mother had to improvise evening dinners. I doubt that any of us children took it in at the time, but many a meal was built, not around beef, veal or lamb or those delicious baked fresh salmon roasts but, for instance, around a sort of salmon soufflé made from canned salmon—then so plentiful and inexpensive, perhaps a dime for a tall can at the grocery store. Or when the main course was baked lima beans, which all in the family loved (except Davy, who wouldn't touch them)—and for Davy macaroni and yellow cheese, which he loved and the rest, my mother excepted, would not touch. In a real way we were a family given to individual food foibles, and my mother indulged us good times or bad.

Such cutbacks may have been minor hardships. But unlike happier, spirited times, such occasions were too often marked by my father's poorly concealed, dispiriting, penetrating gloom: his self-expressed sense of failure.

One painfully embarrassing experience related to hard times occurred when I was 7 or 8. It involved a new pair of shoes my father had brought home for me to replace a worn-out pair that I, deeply aware of the family's financial plight, had quietly repaired myself. My solution for extending the life of the old ones was to tack thin strips of tin over the broken halves of the soles to hold them together. It was my secret. But my parents discovered it. The moment I saw the new shoes, it was a struggle to hold back tears. They were long outdated button-ups—no doubt a bargain buy—that had gone out of style years earlier with the advent of laced shoes. To compound their antiquity, they had raised "bulldog" toes. I could hardly bear to be seen in them.

I have always felt that our family had a rather high degree of resilience, both as a unit and as individuals. And the good times—even good times tempered with problems—far exceeded all others.

In later years when all of us were grown and making our ways in our chosen pursuits, my mother would reflect on the long span of years leading up to them. And she would say that if given the chance to relive her life, she would do it all over again in the same way: the same husband, the same children, the same experiences—hard times and good—yes, and she would cater to the whims of her brood just as she had always done.

I remember her unfailing encouragement, especially to my father. The times may have looked grim to him, prosperity faltering . . . when, for instance, a carefully nurtured real estate deal collapsed, and with it hopes for continued good times . . . and my mother would talk it over with him assuringly and repeat a familiar phrase of hers: "Everything happens for the best." Whether or not he agreed, he would take her hand and clearly feel uplifted.

And Other Days

My four high school years ran their course, and I entered the University of Washington in 1924, pointing toward a degree in journalism.

That was the year, too, when Melvin, my elder brother, left home for New York, to be followed the next year by Davy.

In 1927, the family now reduced in size and no longer needing as much space, we sold our large Capital Hill home and bought a newly built smaller home within walking distance of the University.

Once on campus I, along with other journalism-oriented students, quickly found the haven of all campus havens: the Daily Shack. It was the base of all journalism activity—the Journalism School, faculty and classrooms, as well as the editorial and advertising offices of the *Uni-*

versity of Washington Daily, the campus newspaper, produced by journalism students. "Daily Shack" was a cherished sobriquet carried over from the days when the entire operation *was* housed in shacklike premises; by the time I entered the University it occupied the lower floor of one of the newer campus buildings.

Not until their junior year were aspiring journalism students formally admitted to the School of Journalism. The first two years were directed for the most part to a broad base of studies deemed by then–Journalism dean M. Lyle Spencer and his faculty to be important for the working journalist: English and English literature in various forms and depths, philosophy, psychology, history, economics, basic business law and myriad others.

But the Daily Shack, exuding high camaraderie between and among students and faculty alike, drew me and my colleagues into the fold. Other practical reasons for my being there were that I signed on at once as a reporter-writer on the *Daily* and I landed a small-paying job as campus correspondent for the old *Seattle Union Record,* one of the city's dailies.

With rare exceptions—mostly to take required courses offered only in afternoon hours—I arranged classes and extracurricular activity so that I could leave the campus, however reluctantly, by noon or 1 o'clock to report for work in the real estate office.

A month before graduation, facing what I suppose was typical uncertainty about the future at a time when campus recruitment had not yet become a way with corporations or other potential employers, it was my good fortune to experience rays of sunshine from two directions. One came out of an inspired idea of my own; the other, simply a gift of blessed good fortune.

Deciding to take a moderately aggressive tack, I carefully composed two long-shot job-application letters to two national magazine editors in New York.

One was directed to Henry Goddard Leach, editor of the *Forum,* and this is what it said.

> *Dear Sir:*
>
> *Because I am aware of two possible uncomfortable reactions toward me: that either I am reaching for the moon or I am possessed of an overflowing quantity of youthful effervescence, I assure you that I am perfectly sincere and quite well-balanced in this that I write, namely:*

I should like to work on your magazine, and I apply for a connection with it.

I possess these qualifications: I am supremely ambitious and thoroughly pervaded with the desire to get into the field for which I have spent years preparing. I have ideas; great admiration for Journalism and the writing craft; some ability to write; desire to work; definite plans for the future; some valuable experience in newspaper work; education.

Next month I shall graduate from the School of Journalism at the University of Washington where besides my journalism work I have obtained a good background in American history, politics, sociology and literature. During my time at the University I have spent a year and a half in editorial work on Seattle newspapers.

I am not evolving a dream in the clouds, sir, when I ask: is there any possibility of getting on your editorial staff?

May I hear from you?

> *Yours very sincerely,*

Within little more than a week came a reply signed by Edward C. Aswell, assistant editor.

Dear Mr. Levy:

Unfortunately, there are no vacancies on the FORUM staff and it is therefore impossible for us to give you the encouragement which, it seems to us, you deserve.

> *Sincerely yours,*

The second letter brought me no job, but it established a relationship that one day would open the door to a second career and a brave new life. That letter was directed to Paul U. Kellogg, editor of *Survey Midmonthly,* and this is what it said.

Dear Sir:

In writing a letter such as this, it strikes me the author is tempting two results far afoul of what he has in mind. One is: at this point you might flick the letter into your waste basket and think no more of it; the other: you might read the letter completely, then flick it into the waste basket and think no more of it. To try for a happier outcome, then, I shall be mildly precipitous.

I am acquainted with your magazine, like it and should like to make a connection with it. I am a young journalist intently interested in newspaper work and magazines (of select type).

I am not spouting with youthful effervescence; I have no idea of producing the great American Anything; I am by no means prepared to step into the world and masterfully, though nonchalantly, point out how it should be run. I am, on the other hand, supremely ambitious and thoroughly pervaded with the desire to get into the field for which I have spent many years preparing; I have ideas and some ability to write; and I have (put away for the future) a desire to take part in the development of a new type of newspaper, which will have much of the deliberative qualities of a magazine.

Next month I shall graduate from the School of Journalism at the University of Washington where besides my journalism work I have obtained a good background in American history, politics, sociology and English and American literature. I am not strictly a novice in my field, having spent a year and a half in newspaper work in Seattle. And I have done some creative work.

Is there any possibility of getting on your staff?

May I hear from you?

Yours sincerely,

This was Mr. Kellogg's prompt reply.

Dear Mr. Levy:

That's a rattling good letter of yours, but we have not an opening in sight.

Sincerely,

Receiving such responses—even though no jobs—was enormously soul warming. Before I had an opportunity to really savor the feeling, however, the second ray of sunshine shone on me.

It was at an evening campus meeting of Sigma Delta Chi, the society of professional journalists, into which I had been proudly inducted a year or so earlier. The time: late May 1929, a day or two after the arrival of the replies from *Forum* and *Survey*.

Perhaps there was an angel on my shoulder. For with no preplanning I was seated beside a legendary West Coast newspaperman, William D. (Bill) Chandler, managing editor of the *Seattle Times*. Leaning over at one point, he said to me: "If you don't have another job when you finish school next month, come and see me. We'll have a job for you on the *Times*." It was one of the most beautiful bolts out of the blue that I had experienced in my life. A dream come true.

I called on Bill Chandler at the *Times* before graduation day, Friday, June 14, to assure him that I had no other job. He extended a welcoming hand, introduced me to various editors and asked that I report for work on the Monday following graduation.

It was an arrangement that suited me perfectly, allowing an entire weekend to relax and recharge my batteries, especially as my final university year had been more tiring than any preceding it. It was another "down" time for real estate—I had stayed out of school the entire year of 1928 to cooperate with my father in a multiple home-building project that proved only mildly profitable. My senior year was a mix of classes, study, retaining my post on the *University Daily,* working with my father in real estate and handling a supplementary job that fell into my hands as editor of a community newspaper. It paid a small, but welcome, stipend and could be handled one day a week from early afternoon to midnight.

On Friday the 14th, I had scarcely arrived home from my last day at the university when a call came from the *Times* city desk.

No point in waiting until Monday, I was told. "Can you come to work right now?" I could. I did. And thus begins the heart of this book: my days as a newspaperman in Seattle—the first of what turned out to be my two careers.

Chapter 4

*I*n 1929, three dailies dominated the newspaper field in Seattle, each with a weekday circulation of just under 100,000. In never-ending circulation wars, the morning *Post-Intelligencer* (known best as the *P.-I.*) and the afternoon *Seattle Times* led the field: shifting top position back and forth. The *Times'* smaller, feisty afternoon rival, the *Star,* was a consistent No. 3. The long-struggling *Union Record,* which I had served as campus correspondent, was out of business, victim of failed circulation and inadequate funding after nearly 30 years of trying.

It was an aspiring journalist's good fortune to land on the *Times:* not to savor its tightly conservative political and economic stance, which was to the right of both its rivals, but to join its crack team of editors and writers, including five who have their place in this story: Managing Editor Bill Chandler, City Editor Rudy Block, Assistant City Editor Ed Kamm, Special Writer Marian Badcon and Rewrite Man Paul Gray.

Arriving at the *Times* for my June 14 "inaugural," I learned that my assignment would be night police reporter, taking over the police beat from a man who was leaving the paper. Hours: 4 P.M. to midnight. Salary: $35 a week, a fairly substantial starting figure in those days. To my pleasant surprise, it was raised to $40 within a couple of months. And a good thing, too, since all salaries would be cut progressively on a percentage basis in the coming Great Depression, until mine bottomed out five years later at $28.75. In later years, I would say that I could tell my grandchildren that I at least held a job throughout the worst of all American depressions—which descended in one stroke with the stock market crash on October 29, 1929.

That was the year my personal and family life underwent change. In late 1929 my father closed his real estate business, sold our home and he, my mother and sister moved to Los Angeles. Thus ended the family's near-quarter century in Seattle, which, for the most part, was a happy time. It was a period, too, when the city took a long stride down the road to becoming the metropolis it would be following World War II.

The stock market crash followed a series of telltale rumblings out of Wall Street, starting in mid-summer with periodic reports such as the *Times* carried under a page-one banner headline on August 9: "BILLIONS LOST WHEN STOCKS DROP." And the Associated Press story detailed how a wide-open break in prices carried scores of issues down $5 to nearly $35 a share. It was Wall Street's response to an unexpected increase in the New York Federal Reserve rediscount rate to 6 percent from 5, a step taken to cool securities speculation. The story described the drop as one of the worst ever experienced in Wall Street. But such mid-summer rumblings failed to dampen speculative buying, and the crash came with generally unexpected suddenness.

Ironically, the coming of the Depression led to a promotion of sorts for me.

In cutting expenses, the *Times* eliminated night coverage of the police beat and I advanced to police reporter—*day* police reporter, the only kind there would be from then on (excepting Saturday night coverage for Sunday editions).

It was an era—perhaps little different from eras before or since—when crime and violence were major news. Murders, robberies, burglaries, assaults, gunplay, arrests made headlines. Related attractions included fires, suicides, raids, accidents (automobile and other), escapades and disturbances of most any kind that brought the police into the action.

The focal point for most of it, and home base for the police reporters, was the old multistoried Public Service Building near the Skidroad district, which on its various levels housed police headquarters, Police Court, dry squad (this was still the day of prohibition), press room—shared by reporters from all the dailies—City Jail, City Hospital and City Health Department and its related services.

All of that, plus the City Fire Department and County Morgue, both situated elsewhere, comprised the domain of the police reporters. A press room ticker kept us in continuous touch with fire alarms, recording locations and indicating the severity of every fire call throughout the city.

Rarely was the police beat considered the elite of news beats. But it was one of the most productive, generating an enormous flow of news and unending headlines. It also spawned a fair share of humor and gentle amusement as well as pathos.

As news stories go, this was no earthshaker—its principal characters being a distressed lady and a frog. Yet, somewhat offbeat, it appeared not only in the *Times* but, via Associated Press, in newspapers throughout the West and prompted readers to express themselves in a barrage of telephone calls.

It had a happy ending—and earned a "well done" for me from my editors.

What more could I ask?

This is how it came about.

One of my early discoveries as a newsman was how much creative pleasure there was in probing to uncover news where, on the surface, none seemed to be: generally a matter of digging into casual reports, seemingly casual incidents and casual comments that had the "smell" of something more than casual. From the beginning, this was my response to an everpresent urge to seek the story behind the story. Most often it led to a story of some kind: perhaps a whimsical feature; sometimes a break of real significance.

On that particular day, I "smelled" the makings of a story in a report taken over the telephone by a police report clerk. A woman called appealing for the police to *please* do something about a frog in a neighbor's yard that croaked incessantly, disturbing daytime peace and interfering unendingly with her family's sleep at night. She said a neighbor's young son had caught it and given it refuge in a backyard reflecting pool, where it stayed.

Unhappily for the lady, it was not the sort of complaint that the police took too seriously. Rather, it was the kind that a clerk typed with a brevity born of seasoned boredom and clipped to what was known as "the hook," a clipboard to which many citizen calls made their way. Police reporters, of course, had free access to the hook, as they had to much that went on at police headquarters.

The next step was to call the lady. She felt reassured that the *Times* took an interest in her frog problem and willingly provided additional details. So the story went to the city desk, into the paper and onto the AP wire.

Naturally, the next day I called to check on results and found the poor lady close to tears. The frog was bad enough, she said, but her family had lost more sleep that night than ever. Their phone had rung incessantly with calls from as far away as San Francisco, San Diego, Denver and beyond, some callers commiserating, some merely saying how funny they thought the whole thing was.

There was nothing to do but report the news. Thus, follow-up story No. 1 telling the unexpected turn of events. That, in turn, was carried by the wire service, as was each succeeding story.

With a certain amount of regret because the lady was so nice and so unhappy, but with loyalty to the cause, I determined that there was little to do but check once again and report late details in follow-up story No. 2, mostly that the frog still held its ground—or pool.

Until it all came to an end with the final story reporting that the neighbor, filled with embarrassment, had ordered her son to take his frog into custody, carry it far away and leave it. That done, quiet was restored in the neighborhood. And the lady, by now filled with relief and pleasure, noted that though there were moments of despair, her family thanked the *Times* for what it had done for the cause.

Where is the newsman or newswoman who rejects an opportunity to score a good clean scoop over the opposition? Probably no place but Never-Never Land. For my part, it was one of the premiums in newspapering. But there were times when preserving a scoop was as formidable as engineering it.

In our typical daily operations, rival police reporters shared information on breaking stories—holdups, murders, fires or whatever. However, we respected each other's right to develop and keep private additional facts that put an individual stamp on the story. Never did I consider that such sharing applied to self-generated stories, including those that grew out of the same sources to which my fellow reporters had equal access: the casual reports that made their way to the hook, for instance.

So it was that I detected the hint of something more than casual in a report on the hook one summer day. It was a call alerting the police to the possibility of trouble on the waterfront. Perhaps purposely, the informant's details were skimpy. He said only that bad blood between two unnamed fish company executives seemed to be heating up and that upon leaving their businesses at the end of the day one or both might be armed.

Though something less than a crisis report, it moved the commanding officer to assign a prowler car to patrol the area from time to time for the rest of the day.

All this suggested something worth following. So when my day's work ended at police headquarters, I made my way to the waterfront and the site of possible trouble.

Seeking focus on the affair, I stopped in one of the several large waterfront wholesale fish companies. I knew that it belonged to the family of a high school friend from the past and believed, correctly, that he was now an officer of the firm. Although years had passed since we had seen each other, it was a cordial reunion. Further, he could— and did—provide background and a "feel" for the tension that was building. Only two waterfront firms were involved. Neither was his. But it was common knowledge in the trade that the rivalry between the two had degenerated into enmity that could erupt into a shooting match. Any time. Even today.

With the story starting to take shape in my mind, it now became a matter of waiting to see what, if anything, might occur. And as early evening approached, something did.

Most of the businesses in the area were closed when a man guardedly stepped out of an establishment into the street. Then another from another establishment. They eyed each other from a distance of perhaps 100 feet for what seemed minutes. One drew a pistol, and three thoughts raced through my mind: (1) Standing between them, as I was, I had better get out of the line of fire *right now;* (2) the story was unfolding before my eyes; and (3) I needed an instant plan to preserve it and avoid what to me was unthinkable—handing the story and a next-morning headline on a silver platter to the *P.-I.,* the only paper with a night police reporter and the only one able to capitalize on such a "gift."

Hurriedly telephoning police headquarters, I gave the fastest possible rundown to Captain E. L. Hedges, commander of the night watch, who was not only alert to the significance of a scoop but was friendly to the *Times*.

It seemed only moments until a police car arrived. The adversaries had not changed positions. Nor had a shot been fired. The officers relieved the two of their firearms, loaded them and me into the police car and sped to headquarters, where the men were ushered immediately into the captain's office and his door closed.

Safe so far! And if my luck held I might indeed have a winner.

A considerable part of my luck, I figured, was that my friend George (Conny) Connaughton was covering the night police beat for the *P.-I.* Conny was perhaps 12 or 15 years older than I, moderately rotund, contemplative. Having no competition in his working hours, he was more inclined to immerse himself in a book in the press room than to spend time looking around police headquarters for news, fully aware that if a major story were to break one officer or another would alert him. I was also certain that his favorable standing with his superiors would preclude a serious rebuke—if any—over a missed story.

Nevertheless, I felt I could not afford to let him see me at the police station at such an hour—a dead giveaway that something was up. There was always a chance that he might wander out of the press room to check on whether anything *was* happening—or for sociability. Yet it was essential that I remain until the captain's interrogation ended and I could read the statements of the two fish company executives—statements that were doubtless being taken by a shorthand clerk in the captain's office that very moment. The entire story hinged on it: on knowing that there was an official police record of the matter.

So I played a game of being-there-and-not-being-there until the interviews ended and the captain opened his door and showed me the reports.

Fortunately, there were no arrests, so no names appeared on the police blotter. Further, the reports of the incident remained in the captain's desk for the time being.

No one could say with certainty whether timely intervention had saved a life or prevented bloodshed. But it proved the end of the open breach between the two businessmen, whose hot tempers cooled with their visit to police headquarters.

As evening light faded, I raced to the *Times* editorial office—unmanned at that time of day—wrote a story flavored with waterfront mystery and left it for the city editor to see on his arrival the next morning.

Next day, the *Times'* first edition carried the story under a front-page banner headline that conveyed the right spark of mystery. The effort was a success, notwithstanding what was about to happen in the police press room. As soon as the *Times* story appeared on the streets, *P.-I.* and *Star* editors bombarded their police reporters for details. By that time, of course, the police captain's full reports were available and the other reporters could pick up the pieces. Small consolation for a clear scoop.

One small aftermath: the *P.-I.* day reporter assumed a full measure of anger on behalf of his newspaper and reasoned, correctly, who was responsible. After all, he had paid no attention the day before to what he, too, had seen on the hook.

A man of quick temper, which was sometimes whetted by a sampling or two of the dry squad's latest haul, he walked over to where I was seated at my desk and without a word let fly with his fist. The damage was minimal: a cut lip and mutual embarrassment over his precipitous display of fisticuffs.

He apologized. But thereafter, he and I never enjoyed a cordial relationship. We did continue on speaking terms.

Let it be recorded that Conny Connaughton and I remained friends for years to come. Also that the *P.-I.* later invited me to join its staff, an offer that I declined. And that I continued to cover the police beat the only way I knew how.

---

Chapter 5

*I*t would seem an unlikely source of humor, but the police beat generated many a laugh—and many made their way into the *Times,* illustrated with the waggish sketches that were one of the specialties of its staff artists.

One reliable place to turn for an amusing touch was the Police Court.

I cannot remember even one significant news story that came out of the court (with the single exception of the arrest of an attaché for some sort of malfeasance). But it was a mine of features. Particularly, for my part, after learning from Rudy Block, who had been through it all before becoming city editor, that you could maneuver your own laughs. (Just as I would later pass the formula along to my police beat successor.)

The court, situated one floor below police headquarters, was only slightly "courtly" in appearance. It had the proper appointments: his honor's elevated bench overlooking the clerk's and bailiff's desks, which, in turn, were set apart from the rows of spectator benches by a paling-like enclosure. And to the right, the prisoner's dock, generally peopled by seedy drunk and drunk-and-disorderly offenders. Altogether, the court showed its age.

Presiding, except for an occasional absence, was Police Judge John B. Gordon, a somewhat rotund gentleman of medium height and more than middle age, who often gave the impression of being half weary of, or half amused by, the daily scene before him. Aside from drunk offenders, there was an occasional case of prostitution and a few relatively minor dry law offenses. Aide to the judge in conducting cases was City Attorney Bruce MacDougall, a jovial younger man who enjoyed—and reciprocated—the friendship of the police reporters.

A typical ploy in developing a courtroom feature was either to look over the prisoners in the dock and choose a likely prospect or to consult quietly with City Attorney MacDougall for *his* choice of a prospect—in any case, to put heads together and concoct a tall tale that the prisoner would offer as an extenuating circumstance for his dilemma. Once we were organized, the city attorney would see to it that the prisoner won his reward in the form of freedom, whether the bench was occupied by Judge Gordon or an acting judge.

And so it was with this typical example, which ran in the paper with a two-column sketch of a tipsy gentleman "seeing" a collection of unlikely beasts. The head read: "Mr. Scully, Sans Circus, Stages His Own Parade."

Jack Scully, 42 years old, a laborer, pleaded guilty to a charge of drunkenness in Acting Police Judge James Crehan's court yesterday.

He came from Anacortes Friday to see the circus, he told the judge, and something went wrong with his plans; at any rate, he got drunk.

City Attorney Bruce MacDougall asked him whether he got as far as the circus.

"Not that I can remember," answered Scully.

"Did you see any animals, then, like pink elephants?"

"Did I?" and Scully turned to the judge. "Aw, please, Judge, let me go back to Anacortes where I can make my home brew in peace and know what I am drinking."

Judge Crehan gave him permission to go home.

On another occasion, aware that Judge Gordon was about to leave on a duck-hunting trip, I was party to arranging a bit of Police Court fun at nobody's expense. Before taking off, the judge stepped into the courtroom and scanned the docket. He noted that 15 prisoners, all charged with intoxication, awaited hearings. It was the last court session before New Year's Day.

"Promise to be good this weekend?" the judge asked.

"Yes!" chorused the 15.

"Release them," Judge Gordon ordered the bailiff, no doubt fully aware that he would be seeing some, if not all, in the same place under the same circumstances on January 2.

It was a time before either the medical profession or the general public evinced awareness that excessive drinking might be a medical or psychological problem. So the drink-prone prisoner—if he had a sense of humor of his own—was the object of sport without remorse.

There was the day when Leo Quinn, a gentle, genial court figure with a drinking problem, made personal and court history, all duly recorded in page-one "Leo Quinn, in again, out again" bulletins in the day's succeeding editions.

His initial court appearance of the day came in a morning session, when he won his release with some sort of yarn for the ears of the judge.

Within hours, he was back again facing the judge on his second drunkenness charge of the day. Once again he was freed.

Within hours, he was picked up once more and locked in jail. Court closed for the day and he spent that night in a cell, thus ending an in-and-out record that perhaps was never surpassed.

Sometimes you simply took the facts and blended them into an offbeat story before the case came to Police Court.

Such was one that appeared in the paper under a two-column head reading: "Police Unnerve 'Brewer'; Let Him Drink Own Beer."

The story reported how three police dry squaders, alerted by the unfortunate victim's neighbor, lay in wait during the night for a 35-year-old shingleweaver to return home from a lodge meeting. Unnerved, he asked and obtained permission to take a drink of his own beer in the presence of the police, "to bolster his nerves."

The officers, in plain clothes, told him: "We're police, here to raid your beer."

Offered the hospitality of the house before the trip to jail, the officers noted that they declined, commenting: "The stuff was bottled only yesterday and was pretty green."

When he arrived at police headquarters, the offender posted $100 bail and was released. But 41 quarts of seized beer were held as evidence, 10 gallons of mash dumped.

Sometimes you merely poked good-natured fun at police officers you liked and who loved the publicity.

Thus, a story in the *Times* under a typically amusing sketch and two-column head "Police Officer Fears Boats Behind Prowler Cars Unsafe" focused on a favorite police lieutenant.

> "And why is Lieutenant Hasselblad looking so glum?" asked Police Captain E. L. Hedges at police headquarters yesterday.
> The answer came from Lieut. Gus Hasselblad himself.
> He fears the boats are not strong enough after Police Chief Forbes announced a new "Coast Guard Division" would have boats hooked on behind prowler cars for drowning calls.
> "If there's anything I hate it's getting wet anyplace other than in the bathtub or in a bathing suit. Let's hope the boats will be made of steel, though, so we might borrow one to go fishing in."

Offbeat humor at police headquarters was not all to be found in the Police Court or at the booking desk.

It wasn't necessarily funny to Detective Captain William G. Witzke, but some of the rest of us found it worth a laugh the day that Witzke's office safe went awry and refused to open when the correct combination was dialed.

It so happened that a safecracker of renown was lodged in the top-floor jail. Witzke called on the professional to try his skill—if he would. And he would if left alone in the captain's office to do it. The safe was opened without force or damage.

Ordinarily, you might expect the climax of the story to be an escape—attempted or accomplished. But not so. The prisoner returned to jail chuckling all the way.

One day the press room ticker tape tapped out a fire call in an area that quick reference to the "snitch book" (the listing of telephone numbers by street addresses) showed to be no seat of the rich or mighty. Yet I elected to call a selected number—a residence at least near the problem—likely beating the fire engines to the scene.

"This," I said, "is the *Times*. Is there a fire in your neighborhood?"

"Hell, yes," a harried female voice shot back. "It's in the next room."

Happily, the firemen arrived and doused the blaze with little damage. Of course, the coincidental incident made the paper.

Then there was a time when no story at all was involved. Conny Connaughton, now covering the day police beat for the *P.-I.*, and I were giving a party that evening (jointly, but quietly, with a scholarly young police officer friend who lived in a houseboat on Lake Union). Conny had somehow come to know one or two members of the Stratford-upon-Avon company, playing a week's engagement of Shakespeare in Seattle, and they and several other members of the cast were invited to the houseboat following the evening's performance—of King Lear, as I remember.

Obviously, such a party without drinks was beyond thinking, and I was elected to visit the dry squad, housed on the floor below the press room to seek the wherewithal.

It proved a moment when the dry squad officers were in a benign and friendly mood; they offered—and I accepted—four 1-gallon jugs of pure grain alcohol. Which raised a personal question: how to handle it and what to do with all of it?

We resolved to devote two gallons to the party—which was a complete success; Conny was to take home what was left of that. I would keep the third and present the other to my *Times* colleagues.

That afternoon I walked out of police headquarters, through downtown to my apartment: the two gallon jugs in paper bags, one in each arm.

The next question was what to do with my gallon? And Paul Gray, the seasoned *Times* rewrite man, solved it. He suggested that I buy a washtub, which I did; mix my gallon with a couple of gallons of apple cider and various spices, which I did; and let it all rest for a couple of weeks, which I did.

When the time arrived to sample the product, I took a taste, then another and another. And all it was was spiced apple cider. What Paul had neglected to say was that the mix should have been covered. The alcohol completely evaporated in my warm apartment. And that was the end of that.

Finally, a story that had no more to do with the police beat than that it involved and was written by the police reporter and it took place in his apartment building.

It appeared in the paper with one of those amusing sketches under the two-column head "Moans Bring Near Neighbors Together, But Not For Long." This is what it said.

> Some young man on the first floor of one of Seattle's newer Ninth Ave. apartment hotels suffered considerably at 2 o'clock yesterday morning. And today for the first time each tenant on the south exposure knows his neighbor.
>
> The moon was high when a short deep moan floated into the misty night from the first floor window.
>
> Silence.
>
> Suddenly from a third floor window boomed a sneeze.
>
> And 30 pair of eyes rolled that way.
>
> The moans continued.
>
> In that wakeful, euphoric moment, heads poked out of windows, neighbor meeting neighbor, it became a chatty, conversational interlude.
>
> And the moans continued.
>
> Suddenly, a bucketful of water splashed from an upper window.
>
> "Shut up," commanded a husky voice behind the bucket.
>
> And everyone did, and heads were pulled back. And everyone listened to moans for the rest of the morning.

Chapter 6

There Were Days
Like That

*I*f anything in life is truly chancy, it would be the interplay of forces that affects the intermingling of people and the way friendships are fashioned. A toss of dice in the hands of a tyro would be more predictable—or guessable.

And so it was in my newspapering days, when unplanned, freewheeling relationships influenced the course of my life and when random incidents grew into unforgettable memories.

Among such friends and colleagues who have a place in these accounts were (in no meaningful order)

> Smitty (Harold Smith), one of the *Times'* ace news photographers
> Rudy (Rudolph) Block, a superior city editor and warm human being
> Marian Badcon, friend, who, like others in this book, has already been mentioned
> Paul Gray, rewrite man
> Ed (Edward J.) Kamm, assistant city editor
> Police Chief Louis J. Forbes
> Detective Chief Charles Tennant
> Detective Leutenant Ernie (Ernest W.) Yoris

plus others who move in and out of the paragraphs to follow.

Smitty and I enjoyed an effective, pleasant working relationship from my early days as a police reporter, when he would be dispatched to police headquarters to shoot pictures on developing stories or when he and I would take off on one significant news break or another: a major fire, shooting, robbery or whatever. In those days news photographers used magnesium powder flashes to light their exposures, sending up clouds of smoke which, happily, dissipated quickly. Flashbulbs appeared soon afterward, making the presence of a working photographer much more agreeable to all concerned.

There was no question among those who knew him that Smitty was a very merry zany, and he helped to perpetuate the notion held by many working newswriters that newspaper photographers as a group were a little nuttier than their fellow human beings. Nutty or not, there was another photographer on the *Times* named Smith, who cheerfully went along with a newsroom gag designed to become a feature story and had his name changed legally to *Another* Smith. Perhaps a touch of zany was what photographers needed to get them through the sometimes tense situations encountered in the course of their work.

A man not quite middle aged at the time, of medium height, tending toward chunky, Smitty could keep up a line of irrelevant chatter any time, any place (his speech betraying just a bit of his British beginnings).

A classic Smitty story recalled the time he was photographing Queen Marie of Rumania and her party, who had paid a brief visit to Seattle in 1926. It was a warm day, pictures were being shot out of doors and Smitty was working hard on his assignment.

Taking off his hat, he handed it to Marie with a request.

"Queenie," he said, "will you hold my hat for a minute?"

She did. He completed his job, reclaimed his hat with a "thank-you" and departed. If the incident bothered anyone in the royal party, it was certain that Smitty took it in stride.

One October morning in 1931, Smitty and I were sent out on an assignment that the city editor very much wanted: a poignant picture and story reflecting reaction, Chinese reaction, to a crisis that was unfolding thousands of miles across the Pacific—Japan's invasion of China in an undeclared war and its seizure of Manchuria, which it was hastily restructuring into a puppet state it named Manchukuo.

The surprise assault had stunned much of the world. It was reported in the *Times* at length on October 3, 1931, telling how a Japanese army already in China precipitated an incident at Mukden, bombing and destroying Chinese barracks as a prelude to overrunning all of Manchuria and claiming it for Japan. The act was one in a long series of full-scale aggressions that began with the annexation of Korea by Japan in 1910 and continued until the end of World War II in 1945, when Japan ceded its conquests.

Seattle's Chinese community at the time was dotted with war bulletins, often posted outside food markets and mercantile establishments. Seattle, of course, had a sizeable Chinese population.

The bulletins were scripted in Chinese on large sheets of white paper. What we were after was a small knot of people—three or four or more—eyes directed to the news bulletins. It would be mainly a backside view but, with a deft camera angle, should catch enough of a face or two to suggest anguish.

Certain that we knew the perfect spot, we drove to a small food store on a fairly secluded street on Yesler Hill. And surely enough, there was a small group outside taking in the news.

Our picture and story were shaping up for us. We thought.

From that moment, however, it was all downhill. No sooner did Smitty's camera come into sight, no sooner did I approach to speak than the entire group melted away. No comment. And no picture.

Asked for his cooperation and reassured of our good intentions, the storekeeper merely shrugged.

And so it went, place after place throughout Chinatown. Until, defeated, we retreated empty-handed: I back to the police station, Smitty to the *Times*.

I never knew whether there had been suspicion in the *Times* editorial rooms that such might be the outcome.

Why our mission failed so completely remained a question for me until years later, when I read into the early history of Chinese oppression in Seattle and the Northwest (including western Canada). I learned then what in 1931 I did not know: how shiploads of coolies were brought from China in the mid-1800s—many simply shanghaied—to build the railroads and perform numerous other menial tasks, including hard labor in the mines, only to be shunted off when their jobs were finished and white men wanted the available work . . . how they were victimized, driven from their simple living quarters, out of towns and cities, assaulted and often murdered.

Historian Edmond S. Meany, a longtime professor of history at the University of Washington, tells in his book *History of the State of Washington* (New York: Macmillan Co., 1927) of numerous instances of humiliation and suffering inflicted on the Chinese.

Examples: (1) How, on a September night in 1885, five white men and two Indians climbed an orchard fence in Squawk Valley, about 20 miles north of Seattle, and fired rifles and pistols into tents where 37 Chinese slept. The toll: three Chinese killed, three others wounded. The Chinese had been brought in to pick hops against angry protests by white and Indian hop pickers. All the survivors left the next day. (2) Four nights later, miners in Coal Creek, near Seattle, attacked and burned the Chinese quarters. No killings, though one Chinese was choked and the clothing of 49 burned. (3) Two months later in Tacoma, a short steam blast was the prearranged signal for several hundred white men to gather and "escort" the Chinese out of the city.

The level of anti-Chinese feeling was such, even before Washington gained statehood in 1889, that one Seattle restaurant could advertise as a point of pride: "No Chinese employed."

What Smitty and I unwittingly encountered in our search for a dramatic photograph were the smoldering memories, the distrust that lingered among the Chinese in our midst.

Smitty and I had not seen or communicated with each other for at least 40 years, both presumably unaware of the whereabouts of the other, when one Sunday morning the telephone rang in our home in Glendale, California. It was Smitty calling from Seattle to recall old times, to say that Leah, his beloved wife of long years, had died and that he would like to come and see us.

It was a shaft of bright nostalgic light for me. I urged him to come as our guest, and he promised he would.

He never did.

We learned later that within days of his call, Smitty died.

Marian Badcon was one of the newspaper's all-purpose stars: equally skillful covering stories, writing (speedily and well), working the rewrite desk and filling in as a city desk assistant as called on. Perhaps 38ish, vibrant, attractive, she enjoyed her life as a newswoman with the same high enthusiasm she devoted to her other role as wife and mother.

She was on the rewrite desk one day when I called in with a tear-jerking police beat story that I knew she could turn into a thing of beauty. This, by happenstance, also focused on the Chinese but was a world apart from the wartime story that had engaged Smitty and me.

It was the practice of beat reporters, whether police, city hall, courthouse, federal or other, to write only a limited number of their stories. Rather, as a way of speeding the process and moving news into print, such reporters—along with those in the field working on fast-developing stories—phoned the facts to a rewrite man or woman, whose job it was to put it all together and send the finished product through the appropriate editors and into print. Time and its limitations were always important to an afternoon paper.

Marian, like others in the editorial rooms—certainly City Editor Rudy Block, Rewrite Man Paul Gray and Managing Editor Bill Chandler—was enormously supportive of me. It was as though they had determined not to let me travel into the future anything short of a well-versed newsman.

Instead of taking notes and writing the story, as I expected, Marian determined that this one would be mine from beginning to end. Nudging, cajoling and encouraging, she forced me into a new chapter in my newspaper life—dictating a story directly from notes, a capability I had doubted was within me.

So, with utmost patience, she typed as I dictated, and in the process a useful new facility evolved.

This is how my initial venture into the art came out, featured on page one of the next day's (Sunday's) editions:

> Heavy feet shuffled along Washington Street. A few turned into the Chinese mercantile establishment at 216, past shelves lined with Chinese-labeled jugs of ginger and other spices and through a small doorway into the back room.
>
> Lottery tickets hung against the wall. A sign announced the 2 o'clock "draw." An old Chinese nodded reflectively. Young Lim Ton Wing dipped his brush in the inkpot and hurriedly wrote in Chinese:
>
> "Dear Father . . . "
>
> That was the way Lim Ton Wing, 19 years old, began his suicide note yesterday. Half an hour later his body lay across the carpet of his little green-walled room above the first floor of 216 Washington St., his father's establishment.
>
> He shot himself in the heart because he was ashamed—he had dishonored his parent.
>
> A large photograph of his father, Lim Paik, hung on the wall.
>
> Writing in scholarly Chinese, learned in his native land, Lim Ton Wing detailed his troubles. He had spent $100 entrusted him by his father in a manner other than his father had directed, a translation revealed.
>
> "I am ashamed," he wrote. "I am sorry for my mother in China."
>
> He asked forgiveness. He asked that salary due him from his father be sent to China to his young wife that she might adopt a son to bear his name.
>
> A little knot of Chinese stood near the boy's room as Lim Paik ran in from a nearby shop. The father squeezed through a ring of bystanders. A City Emergency Hospital doctor, kneel-

ing beside the boy, turned and told the father Lim Ton Wing was dead.

Lim Paik slumped in a chair and ran his fingers through his hair.

In those days, the newspapers, including my own, paid attention to suicides. Sometimes they involved people of prominence and thus became stories of significance. More often, the victims were unknowns, and the news was reported in a brief paragraph or two. But they were reported. And it was up to the police reporters to get the facts, which in routine cases were simply gathered by telephone from one deputy coroner or another, all on mutually good terms.

Suicide by gas, it seemed, was most typical, and therein rests a tale.

In my early days I would meticulously phone all the facts to Paul Gray, a veteran on the rewrite desk—all the facts, it turned out, but one. Name, address, circumstances, cause (gas, pistol, poison or whatever), family, suicide note or not, who discovered the body, and so forth.

When gas was the cause of death, Paul unfailingly shot a question back at me.

"How many gas burners were turned on?"

In the beginning, it was a mild irritation because I would have to call the morgue, ferret out and relay the information. It became a point of amusement for my police press room colleagues. As soon as they heard me say "I'll find out and call back," they would chorus at a level a few decibels above sotto voce: "That's Paul Gray on the other end."

Until one day it dawned on me that Paul was deadly serious and had reason to be. If one burner were found open—or even two—it might easily be a death mystery worthy of pursuit. If *all* gas burners in a kitchen range were open and the doors and windows sealed, that meant suicide.

I never bothered to explain the rationale to my fellow newsmen. But I learned another worthy lesson in news reporting: *Don't give up until you dig out all the facts.* And thereafter, Paul got the answer before he could ask.

Ernie Yoris, the detective lieutenant, and I became warm professional friends. Whether he and the other police reporters enjoyed the same relationship I do not know. But he and I got along very well together and we could be mutually helpful. He was a sort of storybook detective: ruggedly handsome, no blabbermouth but willing to share

Adding to the pleasure of my life as a newspaperman, the City Desk encouraged me to seek out and write features that often were embellished with cartoon sketches. This sample plainly goes back to my days as a police reporter.

Police Reporter Views New Cars; Black Maria Is Passe

By the POLICE REPORTER

Until he saw the Automobile Show yesterday the police reporter felt that Black Maria might do the city for another year.

It's such a roomy old wagon. And (sentimentally speaking) police have hauled so many interesting folks in it—bad men, topers, robbers, celebrities, smart men and pert women who happened into the right gambling places at the wrong times, gunmen.

Old Black Maria seemed serviceable and satisfactory.

But today, no more.

With Ash Trays, of Course

Something in a rich maroon, with wind-deflecting fenders and body, low-slung chassis, vibrationless motor, soft cushions and built-in ash trays—that's what Chief of Police William B. Kent should buy to haul his prisoners. The latest creations in cars have them. Most every automobile on the floor at the Civic Auditorium has—except that some are vivid blue or mauve.

And after all, if Chief Kent prefers something besides maroon that would be all right, too. Maroon Maria sounds no better than Blue Maria or Mauve Maria.

Problems Are Lessened

It wouldn't be nearly the problem urging inebriates or other unwilling arrestees into the patrol if a swank 1932 model swished up to police boxes instead of lumbering old Black Maria. And with the clutch pedal almost as unnecessary to the newer machines as billy-clubs to modern patrolmen, the patrol driver would have an extra leg to use in urging recalcitrants into the wagon.

All these things Chief Kent should consider. At least, that's what the police reporter thought about it.

In another pensive moment at the Auditorium yesterday, as he watched the featured Spotlight Reviewers perform from backstage, your reporter sighed and wondered why such a beautiful brunette as that dancer or such a grand blonde as that singer never crosses his path at police headquarters.

information with those he trusted—and more than that, was well trusted by his fellow officers. And by informants, too.

He often cued me in to the right direction on stories I worked on and would fill in a detail or two that made the difference in my perception of a case.

In addition, I learned things from him about police work that were sometimes significant, sometimes merely interesting.

I learned from him the heavy part that tipsters play in police work: that solving a crime might well involve no more than 10 percent police work of the kind people outside the profession normally thought of and 90 percent based on information from informants. Which meant that effective detective work was closely associated with cultivating and maintaining contacts beyond the law.

Another random bit of information learned from Ernie Yoris—and no doubt I'd never have known it otherwise—was about "yen-shee babies." (Yen-shee: an opium derivative.) Of course, he knew narcotics users and he knew from them all about the constipating effects of yen-shee: how users often went for months without an evacuation. And how the day would come when a "baby" would arrive in the form of a big, hard movement. And how that was a matter of happy news among fellow users, who gossiped about it among friends and fellow sufferers.

Then there was an unsavory case involving a patrolman stationed at police headquarters. It had simmered for some time when—with Detective Yoris on the case—it broke wide open, not to be closed for a year and a half, when the offending policeman entered the state penitentiary at Walla Walla as convict No. 14000.

In a public airing of the case, the *Times* reported on March 29, 1930, how "Patrolman Dan Hogan, avowed candidate for King County sheriff at the November election and prominent lodgeman" was dismissed for releasing a bootlegger from jail.

"Hogan, officials said, admitted accepting $200 from . . . a convicted bootlegger and ordering his release from the city jail after serving but 19 days of a 140-day liquor sentence." The story reported that, when questioned by authorities, Hogan admitted taking money from various jail prisoners from time to time. It also noted that the prisoner who was released prematurely was found and returned to jail to serve the remainder of his term.

Detailed by Police Chief Forbes and Detective Chief Tennant to examine all jail records over a period of months, Yoris discovered a number of "suspicious" release orders bearing the patrolman's initials, and all were tracked down. The upshot: the county prosecutor entered the case, filed felony and misdemeanor charges. There were trials, delays a conviction, a prison sentence, further delays and a fruitless last-minute appeal to the governor of the state for a parole or pardon.

What added interest to the case was that Hogan was rarely, if ever, thought of as an "ordinary" police patrolman. He had many friends in town. He had a "presence" at police headquarters, where he often served as booking officer and, as already indicated, one who wrote release orders.

Newsmen on the police beat saw him always meticulously groomed, his blue uniform neat and well pressed, his nails manicured, wearing at least one notably sizable ring. In size and bearing, he could have been a middleweight, if not a light-heavyweight, boxer. He was polite to those he considered equals and could be highly aggressive to those beneath him. One of the first times I saw him in action he was dealing with a very drunk prisoner lying on the floor awaiting an elevator ride to jail. Hogan, offended by some slurred remark, stepped back and delivered the luckless offender an enormous kick in the groin. It was not easy to watch.

It was part of the way of life that police reporters made friends all the way up the ranks: from desk clerks to patrolmen to drivers of patrol cars and city ambulances to motorcycle officers to gold-braided officers to the chief of police and chief of detectives. If a reporter wouldn't—or couldn't—he was not long for the assignment.

One service that fell routinely to police reporters—of all papers, I am sure, but certainly of mine—was to "take care of" traffic tickets for fellow newsmen on the paper. These generally were speeding citations. It was a painless procedure, purely a gesture of friendship, that amounted to handing the ticket to the chief of the traffic division and identifying the unfortunate victim. Thereupon, the wheels of "justice" turned swiftly; the citation was removed from the records and the victim forgiven.

It was, of course, a no-obligation matter involving nothing more than a "thank-you" from the luckless driver—except once, when I took care of a ticket for a gentle, friendly colleague, Al Wilson, an editor with the Associated Press, which was housed in the *Times'* offices. To express his gratitude, he borrowed a copy of D. H. Lawrence's then-banned *Lady Chatterley's Lover* from the vaults of a bookstore where he had familial connections and lent it to me for one week. In the early

1930s, I was likely one of relatively few in Seattle to have read the novel.

My one personal experience with traffic offenses in those years occurred on an early morning drive in my newly acquired Ford to police headquarters and my police beat responsibilities. I was rolling along at perhaps 10 or 15 miles over the prescribed speed limit on a street with sparse traffic when overtaken by a young motorcycle officer who—to my surprise—nodded me to the curb.

Stepping up, citation book in hand, and putting one foot on the running board (which all cars of that vintage had), he looked at me. Paused. Then in a voice midway between surprise and embarrassment, he choked out his greeting, "I didn't know that was you, Levy." He pocketed his citation book, offered a word on the pleasant sunny morning, bade me adieu and we both proceeded on our business.

One day I was in Chief Forbes' office on a news exploration visit when he turned the conversation to what had all the earmarks of a prime, exclusive story. Leaning forward at his desk and lowering his voice, he told me of a tip received by his department via the underworld: a major downtown Seattle bank was marked for a daylight holdup. He named the bank, the day and time of day. He knew the *Times* would treat it confidentially but would want the opportunity to prearrange coverage.

We agreed that photos of a robbery in progress and testimony of newsmen would be invaluable, not only to the *Times* but to the police.

The day and time arrived. My mission was to remain at police headquarters to cover that end of the story, and I waited with subdued impatience for it to unfold.

My fellow newsmen on the *Times* later described the scene to me. There were detectives and *Times* reporters posing as customers all over the bank. *Times* photographers hid at every possible vantage point on the balcony and ground level.

In the end, only one thing was missing. The robbery never came off.

Whether the tip was faulty or the would-be robbers had a change of mind or heart, no one knew. However, the chief, *Times* editors and reporters (including me) agreed that the venture—if more amusing than productive— was entirely worthwhile. Only, better luck next time!

My memory of Detective Chief Charles Tennant was how he warmed up over a period of time, dropped his early reserve and got around to sharing more information with me than I ever supposed he would; indeed, we became quite good friends. That, and his general demeanor—sort of a textbook detective chief: tweed suits, slightly clipped speech, a rack of straight-stemmed pipes at hand, one of them unfailingly in mouth or hand and repeatedly relit with box matches.

Many years later, when my wife and I visited the Sherlock Holmes room in the handsome new Toronto, Canada, Metropolitan Library, it all came back to me in a moment of déjà vu. I had seen a minor version of the Holmes room every time I walked into Chief Tennant's office in Seattle police headquarters.

*A*s the Depression worsened, major fires became part of the way of life in Seattle. It was not epidemic. It merely happened. For the most part, the biggest, most threatening, most spectacular three-alarm fires seemed to occur in the middle of the night—and as police reporter I was there.

Why it fell to the police reporter to cover nighttime fires as well as those that broke out in daylight—all considered part of his day's work, with no added compensation or compensatory time off—I never felt disposed to ask. It was merely accepted by me as one of the requisites of the job.

The closest to a note of explanation for the repeated nighttime interruptions was a complimentary word passed along one day from the city desk: "Colonel Blethen likes the way you cover fires." Colonel C. B. Blethen was the *Times'* publisher, editor, principal owner and descendent of the man who founded the paper in 1896. But we never met and to the best of my knowledge he never expressed an interest in looking me over. It was an anonymity that I felt pleased enough to live with, however, as the Depression wore on and the editorial staff was cut repeatedly in one economy move after another. It seemed well enough to keep my distance in an era when jobs were at a premium.

Besides, for me, the responsibility was never onerous. Once roused from sleep I could scarcely wait to get to the scene of action. I also felt a sense of support from City Editor Rudy Block, a man with a rich appreciation of human relations. It was Rudy who would call and wake me at home; it could be anytime from around 11 P.M. to 3 or 4 A.M. While he had no responsibility for showing up at a fire—and he never did—there was a comforting kind of camaraderie in knowing that he would be as wakeful at his home as I was at the scene until the fire was controlled or extinguished.

In later times, after Rudy Block's departure in another cutback, his successor (whom we will meet later in these accounts) had a different point of view that preserved him from ever having to lose a moment's sleep to a fire. The *Times'* round-the-clock switchboard was instructed to call me upon receiving a three-alarm night alert from the Fire Department. It was never the same.

Even though I came to know precisely what to expect of a late-night telephone ring, I never could bring myself to let it pass without answering. So I experienced many of the most spectacular Depression-time fires in Seattle.

Among all of them, three stand out in my memory, each for a different reason. One was my first night fire. Another, a devastating shipyard fire. The third, a harbor fire in which an Alaska passenger ship met its end.

I felt I was being entrusted with significant responsibility when called one cold midnight a few months after joining the *Times* and dispatched to a fire in a multistory building a couple of blocks from the waterfront. The building was occupied by wholesale mercantile establishments and also used for the storage of merchandise that ranged from department store furniture to stocks of groceries to Eskimo carvings and trinkets—not to overlook equipment and offices of the U.S. Signal Corps.

Among remembered incidents: How more than 20 fire engines and trucks were on the scene in addition to help from two city fireboats that pumped streams of water through fire hoses stretching from the harbor to the fire . . . how adjoining buildings were saved—even though flames rose uncontrolled high in the air . . . how the firemen regarded a reporter for the *Times* with friendly disposition . . . how a couple of them, seeing how ill-clothed I was for such an encounter—dressed in street clothes while tramping through a smoldering lower floor, water pouring from above—suggested that I appropriate a heavy yellow seaman's slicker from a rack in a ship supply store . . . how the fire was extinguished around 2 A.M. and I taxied to the *Times* editorial rooms, wrote my story and left it to be run in the next day's editions.

Possibly most rememberable, however, was my disposition of the heavy yellow slicker. I left it on the city editor's desk with a note attached telling where I borrowed it and asking that it be returned to the rightful owners.

Departing the editorial rooms to catch a few winks of sleep before having to rise again and head for the police station and my 7-to-4 workday—little did I know the measure of my innocence.

Only later would I learn that the first newsman to arrive that morning claimed the slicker as his own. He knew what I would come to realize: the futility of trying to return it and the certainty that it would never be missed in the aftermath of such a fire.

A little after 2 A.M. one October night in 1931 a fire broke out at a shipyard in Seattle's Ballard district—a yard that specialized in building tugs and small work boats—and within two and a half hours flames virtually consumed the entire plant.

As fires went, it was one of the more interesting: the glow as the wooden structure and its contents burned to the ground visible eight miles across the sound; hundreds of spectators attracted to the scene despite rain, strong winds and the predawn hour.

In my personal history of fire coverage, the night was remembable for the birth of an idea I thereafter employed with some frequency: writing a feature—a sidebar story containing incidental information about the fire—to accompany the principal story. In subsequent pondering, I wondered if the sidebars could have been one reason why the publisher of the *Times* liked the way I covered fires.

There were some three acres under roof in the shipyard, which was separated from the nearest fire hydrants by a sandy stretch possibly 600 or 700 feet wide. Arriving on the scene, I noted that lengths of fire hose had been linked together across the sand, and under the high pressure the connections were leaking. The leaking water combined with rain made the sand very wet. And heat from the fire made it very warm.

Therein lay the inspiration for my sidebars. In departing, I saw patches of newly sprouted mushrooms where none had been only two or three hours earlier—thanks to what must have been ideal growing conditions.

That item plus other now-forgotten nubbins made up the first of what was to be a continuing series of night-fire sidebars.

If a disastrous fire can reasonably be described in terms of aesthetics, the last hours of the Alaska passenger ship SS *Alameda* are remembered as a sight of sheer beauty.

The fire started a little past 3:30 A.M. as the ship lay at her waterfront berth. I was there minutes later. The small night crew had been taken off and the ship was being towed from the dock, fuming and smoking, into the harbor as I arrived. I was hailed aboard a harbor patrol boat, which proved a perfect vantage point to see it all and pick up radio talk from the fireboats *Alki* and *Duwamish* as they poured tons of water into the burning ship.

It was a crisp, cold, utterly clear, starlit night in late November 1931: a spectacular setting as the entire ship broke into flames that rose skyward.

It was all over in a couple of hours. The flames were beaten back and she was towed down the bay to Harbor Island and beached on a sandspit—a sad ending for a vessel known as the Blue Ribbon ship of the Alaskan passenger fleet.

A speedster, she established a record that was never in her time successfully challenged, sailing from Ketchikan to Seattle in 41 hours 15 minutes.

Many a time in years past, I had taken refreshing walks along the waterfront, pausing to admire the Alaskan vessels: the *Alameda,* the SS *Alaska,* the SS *Northwestern.* Now their number was diminishing. A year and a half later, the *Northwestern,* too, would meet her fate when she struck a rock near Sentinel Island, Alaska. Her passengers had to be taken off by a rescue ship.

Thus, one transportation era was fading and a new era—travel by air—was moving toward center stage. One airline already was flying small-capacity passenger planes between Seattle and points in Alaska.

And air exploits were becoming major news.

Although it was hardly an "exploit," about that time I made my first airplane flight: a trip over Seattle in an open-cockpit seaplane piloted by Ross Cunningham, a contemporary, friend and fellow reporter on the rival afternoon *Star* and an airplane enthusiast. The *Star,* much like the *P.-I.,* changed police reporters with some frequency, and it was Ross's turn to cover the police beat. He had access to a plane owned by a friend and one day invited me to join him after work for a look at the city from the air—which proved an eye-opening sight.

Once airborne, it took me a few edgy moments to adjust to the continuous vibration of the metal struts that held the plane together and to gain a reasonable degree of poise; it was, after all, the first time

I had been suspended between the open sky and the earth with nothing to do but ride it out.

Then, as I gained courage to look straight down, my first and lasting impression was the abundance of water beneath us. It looked like a massive patchwork of water laced together by stretches of land. And it was strikingly picturesque.

The end of the twenties and the beginning of the thirties was a time when travel by air was nearing popular embracement, but it was not quite there. Charles Lindbergh's New York–Paris flight, which had spawned the new age of the airplane, was a bare two and a half years into history. But air travel   at least in the West—seemed to rest someplace between belief and incredulity.

When the University of Washington's new football coach, Jimmy (James H.) Phelan, was hired away from Purdue University in December 1929 (at the then-history-making salary of $12,000 a year), his arrival in Seattle a few days later via air made front-page headlines in the *Times*. It was announced in a five-column, two-step headline: "COACH PHELAN ARRIVES BY PLANE."

At about the same time the *Times* introduced a column called "Aviation News" as a regular feature.

Again, it was news in Seattle papers, notably the *Times,* in early 1930 when a San Francisco businessman named E. W. Davies, Pacific Coast manager of the Parker Pen Company, speculated in an interview in the city that direct transcontinental airplane service between Seattle and the Atlantic Seaboard would bring Seattle within two days' travel time of New York. And, he said, it was likely to happen "in the near future."

Of course, Seattle was far from the only place in the nation where air news was big news, but for reasons of geography it held an edge over much of the rest of the country—particularly as the first nonstop transpacific flight was yet to be made and a number of known (and unknown) airmen were champing to make it. Included were such names as Bernt Balchen, Roger Q. Williams, John Henry Mears, Wiley Post and little-known Hugh Herndon, Jr., described in print as a wealthy New York youth.

When, in April 1931, *Asahi,* one of the leading newspapers of Osaka and Tokyo, posted a prize of $25,000 for the first foreigners to make a nonstop Pacific flight between Japan and the USA, the race was on. The newspaper specified that if the contender started from the United States, he must take off someplace south of Vancouver, B.C.

The offer of the prize was a front-page banner headline story in the *Times*.

Two Texas flyers, Reg L. Robbins and Harold S. Jones, took off from Seattle for Japan on July 8, 1931, only to be forced down the next day near Nome.

The big break came on October 4, 1931, when American flyers Clyde E. Pangborn and Hugh Herndon, Jr., took off from Samashiro Beach, Japan, to fly to Seattle and they made it with a plus. They carried fuel for 4,800 miles for a flight of 4,465 miles. They landed in the eastern Washington city of Wenatchee on the morning of October 5, coming in without landing gear, which they had abandoned en route to lighten their load. The $25,000 prize was theirs.

It was a big day when they came to Seattle for a whopping downtown parade in their honor. Schools closed for the day.

It was a long way from fires, ships and planes when it was announced in December 1930 that the Chicago Civic Opera was coming to Seattle to present a series of five operas. *Times* theater-music critic Richard E. Hays wrote that it "will be the most notable season of opera in the history of local music." Ticket prices were scaled from a low of $1 to a high of $6.

Promotional excitement rarely let up between then and the smash opening night three months later.

And the "smash" included the police reporter.

The masterminds on the city desk, knowing an offbeat story when they engineered one, determined that I would attend and write a commentary/review as seen through the eyes and ears of the police reporter. The opera: *La Traviata*.

Happily, I still had a tuxedo remaining from an investment made in my senior year at the University.

The typical playful cartoon that accompanied the story the next day not only showed the reporter in faultless evening attire but indicated that he was accompanied by a fetching, also faultlessly attired, female companion. A cartoonist's dream to be sure! While the reporter was provided a ticket—and even taxi fare—to the event, there was no expense allowance for a post-opera evening on the town, and the reporter was much too broke to tackle it without subsidy.

Appearing under the head: "Times Change Strangely; Police Reporter Attends," my review reported on the evening, starting with Act I, and this is an excerpt:

> The dramatic critic will tell you, probably, of a stirring overture magnificently played; of a colorful setting; of vivacious and comely ladies; of charming voices. He may even speak of it as a "riot of color," although we of the police beat have long since discarded the phrase.

> And of the plot . . .

> Violetta is the heroine, you know, who is really much in love with Alfredo, who is awfully in love with her, too. At first she pretends she doesn't care for him—womanlike, you see. She fears she's not his type. But by the time the second act has rolled around love has conquered all. The Romans had an expression for it: Amor omnes vincit.

Readers who had interest in a more insightful review of the opera—and the evening—were provided column on column of reading material all the way from the (regular) critic's review to what each of the hundreds of fashionable ladies in attendance wore. And how a driving rain fell as the audience of 4,500 departed.

Chapter 8

Almost any day in the life of the police reporter was a mix of happenings, from major events that made big news to little events that often had no news value whatsoever but added flavor to the goings-on. Both made lasting impressions on this reporter.

Such was the case of Detective Lieutenant Martin Cleary and his hospitality.

As with most detectives on the force, I enjoyed a friendly relationship with Martin. (We generally called our police associates by their first names or nicknames.)

He was an affable, hardworking detective: rarely, if ever in my experience, involved in a major case but an all-round good journeyman operative. And he never failed to let me know how he appreciated the way I mentioned him and his working partner, Lieutenant Scrafford, in stories about significant cases they had a hand in. (It was my practice, followed also by many colleagues, to name the officers involved in such cases, partly because it contributed something to a story, partly as a considered touch of personal cultivation.)

One day, Martin invited me to join him for an after-work drink or two of beer at his home. It was an expression of friendship.

Of course, I accepted—even though I was no beer drinker and preferred always to bypass home-brewed prohibition beer. Martin, however, could be expected to rank a cut or two above ordinary home-brewers since, as he would recall in reflective moments, he had been a professional bartender in earlier days, until prohibition closed the saloons and he joined the police department.

We were getting along very well in the living room of his home, the conversation flowing satisfactorily, each of us downing one bottle of homebrew after another. Until Martin grew cosy in his confidences and shared his new brewing secret—fast aging. "You will find this hard to believe," he said, "but I made this batch only the day before yesterday. It's been aging ever since under running water in my bathtub."

I felt an instant psychological—as well as physiological—affect.

I believed.

Excusing myself with assurances of a delightful afternoon . . . and conveniently "remembering" another appointment . . . I left hurriedly. The next few minutes were a race against time to get to my own dwelling, where I could disgorge Martin Cleary's homebrew. Let it be recorded that I made it, and not two seconds too soon.

Our professional relationship continued. But never again did I partake of so much as a nip of Martin's hospitality.

One summer day, two successive reports came into police head-quarters. A black bear was rummaging in a backyard garbage can in one residential district. And another black bear was doing the same in a yard a mile or two away. Both homes were within hailing distance of a wooded area.

But bears—black, brown, cinnamon or any other stripe—*never* invaded the city. It took the second call to erase police incredulity enough to have a rifle-armed team of bear hunters dispatched to the scene.

Surely enough, the officers returned with one downed bear.

That much was news, reported in the day's editions.

The next day, after the animal had been properly dressed, one of the officer-marksmen offered me a bear meat roast, which I cheerfully accepted with thanks.

Having neither the resources nor the talent to cope with it, however, I thought of Marian Badcon, probably as good a cook as she was a newswoman. Neither of us had tasted bear meat, so she accepted the gift and I accepted her invitation to share it the coming Sunday with her, her husband and two young sons.

The companionship was excellent. But the pièce de résistance was something else.

I cannot say whether it was Seattle black bear or black bear from anyplace, but all of us voted the roast—handsome to look at—as about equal to a stringy third-rate cut of undernourished beef.

It would have been a constructive solution had the police simply shooed the bear back into the woods.

Then there was the day police rescued a near-drowned man from the bay. Rushed to City Hospital, he revived. The police reporters, having nothing better to do at the time, determined to follow the case to its conclusion.

It turned out that the victim, while able to speak, spoke no language familiar to any of us.

Judging from his wrinkled, coppery face and small stature, we determined that he was an American Indian. And remembering that the Police Court bailiff, Mr. Perkins, had long professed command of Chinook, we sent a hurried call to the Police Court, on the lowest floor of the building, urging him to rush to the top-floor hospital.

That was where I learned—and would remember ever after—the presumably Chinook sentence that Mr. Perkins uttered: "Hi-lo! Kumtux Chinook wa-wa?"

Whether it was pidgin Chinook or pidgin English or neither, it drew one word of response, which all of us gathered there affirmed was "Juni."

Surely, we agreed, that was the man's name.

Now that we had a name for him, the rest of the newsmaking was simple. The story of his last-moment rescue from the cold waters of Elliott Bay and his recovery—all seasoned with a bit of Indian mystique—made its way into the *Times*.

Ultimately, Juni left the hospital, surely unaware of his moment of recognition in print. Where he went, none of us knew.

My face-to-face encounter with Harry Stone, described in the October 1, 1930, *Times* as a "notorious Pacific Northwest outlaw with a price on his head for murder" who was being sought as one of the six submachine gun bandits wanted for the $44,300 robbery of the Citizens National Bank at Everett, was assuredly an anticlimax for both of us.

He had been captured, wounded in the arrest and, at our meeting, was in bed in a cell at City Hospital, manacled hand and foot.

All I wanted was an interview with a famous outlaw.

With a police guard standing by, I stepped up to the open cell door and addressed him.

The instant he heard the words *"Seattle Times,"* he performed a feat that won my admiration, ending an interview that had barely begun.

Manacled as he was, he managed to take hold of a bedpan on a table beside his bed and hurl it directly at me. Fortunately, I sidestepped it.

He remained where he was as I walked down the hospital corridor deciding "Perhaps another time, but not now."

One experience I welcomed, but after a single try determined nevermore: a ride in a City Hospital ambulance speeding on an emergency call.

The driver, a tall, lanky young man of forgotten name, received the call as we were chatting in the underground garage shared by police cars and ambulances and asked if I would care to join him. I scrambled onto the seat beside him and we were off.

Racing through downtown streets, siren blasting, we traveled through the middle, right and left sides of the streets. I had a moment's flash that our first near-encounter was going to be our (my) last as we drove squarely for a streetcar heading toward us. But the ambulance driver knew exactly what he was doing and coolly veered outward and onward.

He drove with calculated skill, missing automobiles, pedestrians and non-stationary streetcars by what I felt was inches, until we arrived at the scene.

The cause of the call was a pedestrian whose injuries, fortunately, proved minor and he declined a trip to the hospital. "Fortunately" not only for him but for me. We drove back to the garage at normal speed.

I doubt that the driver ever knew what an excruciating trip it was for his initially willing, nay eager, companion, though he may have wondered why I never again joined him on an emergency call.

A relatively small home fire broke out one afternoon just in time to make a page-one headline story in the last edition: rememberable for what could be called special circumstances.

Hurriedly gathering details from the press room by phone, I luckily reached the battalion chief commanding the fire units at the scene. Everything was under control and he was able to take time to provide the essentials, including not only names and addresses but dramatic details. Battalion chiefs were almost unfailingly reliable reporters with a good sense of news values, and he was no exception.

The heart of the story, which as he told it I could plainly see pointed to a headline, involved a dramatic rescue by a young mother, who had carried her two small children to safety just before the firemen arrived. Then, as though it were an afterthought, he concluded: "The family is Negro."

On the scale of news values then governing all major Seattle newspapers, *that*—the color of the people involved—could reduce news interest in the story to a minimum. It was common newspaper practice then to characterize principals in stories, if black, as, for instance, "John Doe, a 35-year-old Negro bricklayer (or painter or clerk or whatever). . . . " No doubt was left as to skin color even among professionals—doctors, lawyers or whatever they might be.

The only other reporter in the press room at the moment was Sam Groff of the *Star,* a quiet, bright, highly respected man older than I, who had a reputation as a very good newspaperman and a very good comic cartoonist.

His deadline was at hand, too, and I shared every detail.

It took only a moment for us to agree to strike a blow for humanity and call the story in to our office omitting only the battalion chief's concluding words.

It made a front-page headline in our last edition.

About an hour later I received a call from my city desk to tell me what they assumed I would have had no way of knowing: When a photographer went out to shoot pictures for the next day's editions, he found that the family was Negro. So, no pictures and no next day follow-up.

Both Sam Groff and I felt an inward sense of warmth and satisfaction.

---

Chapter 9

*The Adventures
of Ma Kennedy and
Whataman*

*W*hen newlywed Minnie (Ma) Kennedy
and her shy bridegroom, Guy Edward Hudson, made a quiet entry into
Seattle in the summer of 1931, they had never heard of a waitress
named Queenie or the police reporters on either the *Seattle Times* or
the *Seattle Post-Intelligencer.*

It is doubtful that they ever did hear of Queenie, at least by name.
But they soon came to know the two police reporters who, with Ma's
unsuspecting collaboration, endowed the groom with a name he would
bear long into the future—"Whataman."

During the 1920s and into the 1930s, newspaper readers and radio
listeners across the country had been able to follow the closely reported
adventures and misadventures of Evangelist Aimee Semple McPherson
and her mother, Minnie (Ma) Kennedy.

Aimee McPherson, of course, was the star. One of the most publicized women in America at the time, a peerless preacher and fund-
raiser, lovingly called Sister by her congregants and other admirers, she
built her famed (and costly) tabernacle, Angelus Temple, the Church
of the Foursquare Gospel, in Los Angeles. And it was she who raised
the money for it.

Ma, if less glamorous, was not far behind. For years, she was
Aimee's close companion as well as co-owner, with her daughter, of
the Temple, which she served as business manager. She also was pos-
sessed of much of the same talent for attaining public attention.

And so it was that Ma Kennedy and Guy Edward Hudson eloped,
stealing out of Los Angeles and driving to Longview, Washington,
where they were married in a moonlight ceremony in a public park on
a late June night.

The news media learned of the marriage and saw to it that it received proper national attention. But not one reporter could find out where the happy couple had gone after that. Until . . .

Since the story—though published repeatedly—has never until now been fully or correctly told, it seems appropriate to pause in this narrative for a word from perhaps the last remaining principal: the *Times* police reporter who was there.

At the time, a reporter named Phil Calhoun (called Cal by his colleagues) was covering the police beat for the *P.-I.* He was an excellent newsman who later would go on to play highly significant roles in the *Time/Life* news organizations. He was a contemporary, a friend, a wit— and the only opposition newsman in my working experience whose information on stories—whose facts—I would accept without seeking to confirm them for myself. We nevertheless worked independently, and I am sure that if either could have scored a good clean scoop on the other, he would not have hesitated. But we never did—or could.

So on that early July day, Cal and I left together, as we often did, for an expeditious lunch in the Frye Hotel Coffee Shop two or three blocks from the police station.

We barely had a chance to scan the day's menu when our favorite waitress, Queenie, approached our table. She was a buxom young woman who delighted in our repartee—as we did in hers. She was not pretty but her broad Irish smile warmed any occasion. We never knew her real name. We simply decided one day to call her Queenie, and she always responded. Nor did she know our names. She knew only that we were police reporters for the *Times* and the *P.-I.*

Leaning in a bit, she said, "Do you know who that couple is at the table back there?" indicating the direction with a slight nod of her head.

We didn't.

"That," she continued, "is Ma Kennedy and her new husband."

I cannot remember that we ever got around to ordering, let alone eating, lunch that day. We simply rose unobtrusively, walked calmly to the table where the Hudsons were lunching and greeted them by name.

As the news accounts correctly reported, surprise was the word for their reaction. And that surprise increased when we introduced ourselves as members of the press.

From that point on, the story of the encounter told in newspaper files now more than half a century old, in magazine reports and in published books is substantially the way it happened.

Ma parried a bit and smilingly suggested keeping the discovery a secret: "You just go along and pretend you haven't discovered us," while her husband rose from the table and started walking out, pleading with both reporters who followed him: "I wonder if you would give me just a little time? You see, I have a bad cold and can't talk much. I must have got it staying indoors so much. This is the first day I've ventured out in daylight since our marriage last Saturday night. There have been so many of you fellows trying to find us."

As he departed the restaurant, we returned to Ma, the key member of the twosome, who was finishing her dessert. And a fairly lengthy interview with her took place.

"Pa's got a cold," she observed, "but I can talk." And she did.

"How did I happen to marry Mr. Hudson? Because he is the first man who ever came to me without that 'a little cottage with flowers all around'—you know the rest of that one. I told him I wanted to carry the Gospel. He urged me to do so. 'Work,' he said. Then I became interested in him.

"This honeymoon is the happiest moment of my life. I could travel on and on like this forever. I'm soaring in the clouds.

"The Reverend [he affected the title at the time] . . . The Reverend Mr. Hudson! Whataman!"

And those last five words, taken in by both Phil Calhoun and me, became the lead of my front-page story in the *Times* that day: a line that, thanks to wire service reports, was repeated in news accounts throughout the nation and would live longer than Ma Kennedy.

What the press accounts and recorded history failed to reveal was the part that Queenie played . . . and the presence of not one, but two reporters. Minor though it may seem, had it not been for Queenie, neither Cal nor I would have made our "discovery"—again proving the significance to newsmen (as to detectives) of cultivated contacts. The newlyweds would have gone their way, to be found at another time and place, possibly of their own choosing. And the enduring name "Whataman" might never have been born.

To explain Queenie's absence from the accounts: As told earlier in these pages, under time pressure, I phoned the details to a rewrite man, who put the story together for publication. The *Times* rewrite man, taking the facts from me, dramatized the incident a bit, telling how the newlyweds "were quietly nibbling lunch today in a secluded corner of a downtown coffee shop when in walked a reporter who, after one look at them, interrupted their tête-à-tête with: 'Good afternoon, Mr. and Mrs. Hudson. And how are the newlyweds?' "

Of course, the afternoon *Times* had the news break; the *P.-I.*, with Cal's account, did not appear until the next morning. By which time the story had been absorbed by newspaper readers and radio listeners everywhere.

The honeymooners' joy of July 1931 would, unhappily, erode step by step over a relatively short span of time.

Within days, a prior Mrs. Guy Edward Hudson, alerted by news reports, came forward in southern California to announce that she and her husband, the self-same Mr. Hudson, had never been divorced. She made it clear, however, that she would not mind giving him up. She sued for divorce; Ma Kennedy Hudson meanwhile sued in Los Angeles to have her marriage annulled as a step toward a proper second marriage to Whataman. The objective accomplished, she and Hudson remarried.

Ultimately, however, the couple had a falling out, in the full light of publicity, and their second—and final—marriage ended in divorce.

Ma Kennedy died in Los Angeles in 1947, about three years after the death of her daughter Aimee, also in Los Angeles.

But the name Whataman lived on.

And Other Names in the News

The saga of Aimee Semple McPherson and Minnie (Ma) Kennedy, unveiled in story after story involving incident after incident, was news of a kind that the press almost universally considered newsworthy: the *New York Times* no less than the *Los Angeles Times*, the *Seattle Times* and hundreds of papers in between.

However, it still was a time before abundant, swift air travel had become a way of life, with personalities flying in and out of cities. The presence of a "name" visitor in Seattle was unfailingly newsworthy. Such stories appeared in the news (not departmental) columns along with other local, regional, national and international news.

In the staff-short days of the Great Depression, such interview assignments were passed around to reporters covering beats as well as to the more freewheeling general assignment reporters. And I, of course, had my share.

Among the interviews with personalities that fell to me, two are remembered, not for imperishable words spoken on the state of their art or for their views concerning those troubled Depression times or for forecasts or retrospections, but for unobtrusive moments that revealed how "human" both were beneath their mantles.

One was Madam Ernestine Schumann-Heink, who had attained fame as the world's foremost opera and concert contralto; the other, Alfred Hertz, equally renowned as a conductor of symphony and opera.

The interviews took place at different times in the very early 1930s.

Schumann-Heink, then in her 70s, was in Seattle on a final-final tour, which, she made clear in a guards-down moment, was important to replenish her diminished finances. Her star was descending, and she knew it (though she was yet to make one more appearance with the Metropolitan Opera, in 1932, and would appear in the motion picture *Here's to Romance* in 1935).

The interview took place in her suite in the New Washington Hotel, once the city's class hotel, now a little seedy though perfectly respectable and favored by some travelers.

I recall that the interview went well. Schumann-Heink was good-humored, buoyant and responsive to questions. Her sense of humor was perhaps a characteristic that accounted for her great success as the star in the early 1900s of a comic opera, *Love's Lottery,* written especially for her.

Soon, however, she began to reflect on problems she was experiencing with members of her family. At the time, she lived in San Diego and so did they.

Her mood changed.

Until she suddenly stood and laughed, "Ach, crazy Schumann-Heink, she talks too much."

And the interview ended.

I went to Seattle's Union Station one evening to meet and interview Alfred Hertz, who was arriving by train from San Francisco to make a guest appearance as conductor of the Seattle Symphony Orchestra.

Hertz was a man of rich musical distinction. He conducted at several opera houses in Germany before coming to the United States to join the Metropolitan Opera, which he conducted from 1902 to 1915. There he introduced Wagner's *Parsifal,* Richard Strauss's *Salome* and *Der Rosenkavalier* and Humperdinck's *Königskinder* to the United States and conducted the premieres of several American operas. From 1915 to

1930, he was conductor of the San Francisco Symphony Orchestra and had just taken over as conductor of radio's famed Standard Symphonic Hour.

No other newsman was at the station to meet him, but a small group of Symphony representatives and others were on hand as he stepped onto the platform. It was clear that they had information to share with the maestro before I could step up to meet him.

Hertz, a medium-smallish man with a full beard, clearly had something more than casual on his mind. He stood for a brief interview, then revealed the problem that beset him.

When the train had stopped in Portland before the last leg of its journey to Seattle, he and his wife had stepped off for a brief stroll. Then came the call, "All aboard." He made it back on the train. But Mrs. Hertz didn't. At that point, a couple of Symphony greeters came up to tell him they had been on the telephone with Portland. Mrs Hertz was all right and would arrive in Seattle on a later train.

With that, our interview ended.

Hertz turned and started to walk away, musing: "I wonder what my wife will say."

Chapter 10

Farewell, Police Beat

After two and a half years, the time approached when I would leave the police beat for new responsibilities.

Not that I ever tired of the role of police reporter: every day had been a new adventure. But sensing that City Editor Rudy Block and his city desk assistants were grooming me for a change, I saw no reason to resist a step up in the ranks.

For one thing, they were encouraging me to write more and more of my own material, including straightaway news stories, features and mood pieces. And that was refreshing experience.

My first new responsibility was in the somewhat elevated role of general assignment reporter. Which meant working on a variety of stories, as assigned by the city desk, depending on how the news of the day would break.

Looking back from the vantage point of later—much later—years when general assignment reporters on metropolitan newspapers could be involved for days, perhaps weeks, in researching and writing *a* story or brace of stories, it was clear that the deepening Depression years afforded no such luxury. For the most part, a reporter on the *Times* who was involved in anything short of a blockbuster had to limit the time devoted to any story since he would likely have others at hand to shepherd. Or, as in my case, he might have a standing assignment to mesh with the rest of his day's work.

For me, it was general assignment plus the federal beat: a beat so far less demanding than police that it could be dispatched within a couple of hours a day.

If an assigned story happened to be especially complex, it behooved you to devise a formula for handling it. And no excuses, please.

One such early assignment that fell to me turned out, by the grace of good fortune, to succeed beyond expectation—or hope. It was a story dealing with an Interstate Commerce Commission railroad-rate hearing to determine shipping rates for live Midwest-grown hogs. I doubt that the city desk recognized at the time what a maze I would walk into when told to stop at the Olympic Hotel, where the hearing was in its first day, get a story, then go on to the federal beat.

The economics courses taken in my University days had not prepared me for instant understanding of a case that had entailed lengthy preparation by attorneys and other spokesmen for Northwest meat packers on one side, Midwest swine growers and meat packers on another, grain growers and railroads, all presenting testimony for and against then-prevailing rates for shipping livestock from the Midwest to Seattle.

The solution, for me, was one that is commonly followed by practiced newsmen: make a quick judgment of one or more likely informants and turn to him, her or them for input. You can quickly appraise the quality—the objectivity—of such a one. If you've hit the jackpot, as you hoped, you are "in." If you've missed, you turn to other informants.

The railroad attorney to whom I first turned proved to be a bonanza, as were others with whom I consulted. Although each had his own stake in the case, all were uniformly objective. In an hour or so, including a little auditing of witnesses on the stand, I had a story, complete with names of participants, the burden of their testimony and a clear idea of the competitive stakes.

The hearings and the ICC's ultimate decisions were of high importance to the packing industry in both the Midwest and West, to hog raisers, grain growers and the railroads—and they knew it. The hearings were equally important to consumers, particularly in the Northwest. But it was safe to say that relatively few were aware of them or of the Damocles Sword suspended over the pricing structure. (These were days before public relations and information specialists were on hand with their expertise.)

How to tell such a story in terms of general interest and keep it from landing in the back pages of the paper, where fewer readers were likely to take it in!

The solution appeared to be to bring the consumer—whose concerns were not being argued in the case—to center stage. Thus it was written and thus it appeared on page one of all the day's editions, leading with these words:

> Mrs. Seattle Housewife, who buys the pork chops for her family, was the lady behind the scenes at the Olympic Hotel today as Northwest meat packers told two Interstate Commerce Commission examiners from Washington, D.C., they face busi-

ness ruin if meat shipping rates are lowered from the cornbelt to the Coast, and Midwest meat packers replied that their own business suffers under present rail rates.

Packers, railroad men and economists attending the rate hearing referred to Mrs. Seattle simply as "the consumer" who pays the freight ultimately. [And the story continued with details of the proposed and contested rates and testimony on the varied complex issues.]

Three more days of hearings followed, all covered in considerable detail, all appearing on up-front news pages.

"And in the middle of the fight," reported the final day's story, "hovered the shadow of the attractive Mrs. Seattle Housewife, the consumer, for whose attention both sides are fighting."

Whereupon the hearings adjourned to San Francisco, with no decisions expected for as long as a year or more.

Breadlines became a way of life for down-and-outers in the Depression. One day I was assigned to join a breadline and report on the way it was.

That afternoon, dressed in the oldest, weariest clothes I had, I walked through downtown streets to the Skidroad area and embarked on the story, which ran on page one the next day under the head

ROAST BEEF! UM!

* * *   * * *

Breadliners Eager

And a sketch of down-and-outers waiting in line.
And a byline.
And this, in part, is what it said.

They say the Washington Street breadliners are going to have roast beef and brown gravy this week—and curried lamb and rice.

And—you may believe one who has been in the breadline there—that's news!

Mulligan stew . . . beans . . . bread. Multiply it by seven and you have a rough idea of the main—and only—course on a Washington Streeter's weekly dinner menu. Only, when you have stew you don't have beans and when it is bean night you get no stew. You always can count on the bread. But you take it without butter, or you don't take it at all.

Some of the men think roast beef may be on tonight's menu. Some of them were a little disappointed it wasn't there last night. But it wasn't, for last night mulligan stew ruled the rotund aluminum vats on the second floor at 79 Washington St., where about fifteen hundred men filed in and out for two hours. The roast beef and curry have been promised; that's why the men are expecting it.

The reporter wondered what you get to eat down there. One of the men around the Skidroad had told him stew.

"But what else?" the reporter wondered.

"Well, sometimes beans."

"Yes," asked the reporter, "and what else?"

"Stew."

The line forms at 4 o'clock outside the Volunteers of America Building at Washington Street and Railroad Avenue: Old men, young, white, brown, black and yellow. As you step inside the door you show your work card, issued by the Central Registry for Homeless Men at 213½ Second Ave. S. No card, no food.

Then you march upstairs to the second floor. You show your card again to a man who punches it. You file past the food vats. A server sploshes a plate full of stew into a granite dish and hands it to you. Another server gives you a tin spoon about two sizes larger than your grandmother's biggest serving spoon.

You sit down at one of the numerous long tables, where little piles of five slices of bread are set before each man. . . .

Besides the varied dinner menu promised for this week and weeks to come, cream and sugar are to arrive for the coffee. Volunteers of America workers, who receive the rations from county supplies, announced the good news.

It was at 79 Washington St., too, that the reporter learned the true value of a cigarette. It was during the nightly prayer meeting conducted by Volunteers of America, where the men spend an hour or more before filing up to that same second floor to sleep; where they join in community singing—"Since Jesus Came Into My Heart" or "Throw Out the Life Line" or other hymns.

The reporter squeezed onto a bench beside a middle-aged little fellow in overalls and frayed coat. The man was rolling a cigarette, carefully, almost tenderly. He held it securely as the reporter shifted the bench a little.

On the walls about the room, the reporter noticed, were many signs—"God Bless You, Come Again," "All We, Like Sheep, Have Gone Astray" or "Neither Do I Condemn Thee; Go and Sin No More."

Again the reporter glanced at the little man rolling the cigarette. The tobacco, he observed, was powder-fine, like gathered "dregs" from many tobacco cans; the paper was a torn square of wrinkled brown wrapping paper. The little man hadn't smoked all that day.

General assignment was a definite step up from the police beat. Here you worked on a multiplicity of stories of varying degrees of importance beyond those "belonging" to beat reporters. The base of operation was the *Times'* city room, the principal editorial department, where I had my assigned desk and typewriter and wrote my stories. There was immediate access to the city desk. And I no longer had to report for work at 7 A.M. Now it was 8 o'clock.

And so it went for nearly a year, when the most prestigious of all beats was assigned to me: the courthouse.

The County City Building, known also as the King County Courthouse, was a block-square, modern, multistoried structure that housed the state's two largest entities of local government: King County and Seattle. Here were the mayor, city council and other municipal offices, as were the board of county commissioners (the county's five-member governing body), county clerk, auditor, treasurer, prosecuting attorney and battery of assistant prosecutors and all other functioning bureaus, its many Superior Courts and judges, the sheriff and, on the top floor, the county jail.

Each daily paper regularly assigned two reporters to the building, one to cover the courthouse, the other the city beat. Covering the county for the *P.-I.,* the chief competitor, was a contemporary, a veteran on the beat named Forrest Williams: reasonably friendly but taciturn, altogether a worthy competitor and a challenge to step lively. Each newsman had his own office and telephone. There was scarcely any exchange of information from one to the other.

As the seat of government in the state's most populous county, the King County Courthouse was also the largest and most demanding of beats for the reporter who covered it, no matter which newspaper he represented. ("He" was correct in those days when, unlike times to come, newspaper reporting and editing were broadly considered "man's work." There were exceptions, of course: one, the variously named "Society" or "Women's" pages, which were written and edited by women; another, the sometimes female star who made her mark, such as Marian Badcon of the *Times*.)

Yet, the courthouse assignment was, for me, another round of high pleasure. There were various reasons for this, not the least in coming to know that I could preside with a sense of assurance over the most complex beat of all. Plus the daily experience of dealing with key people in key positions and corralling news of unmistakable significance to the community at large.

You developed your formulas for keeping up with, or on top of, the wide-ranging courthouse news. Each day, for instance, you calculated which of the cases on the court calendar appeared worthiest of attention, having a pretty good idea that one court attaché or another would keep you from blanking out if you missed. And you had ways to keep abreast of the daily filings of civil suits and criminal complaints: aware that some canny attorneys who preferred anonymity for their clients would file papers with the county clerk bare moments before the office closed for the day; others, by prearrangement with a favored reporter or newspaper (which could be you and yours—but not always) might file at a time of day most strategic for the paper of his choice.

You worked out a pattern for touching base with the county commissioners—who combined administrative and executive responsibilities—and for covering commission sessions; much the same with the prosecuting attorney and his key deputies, with sheriff's deputies and others.

Court trials and criminal actions worthy of full-time attention would, except in rare situations, be covered by special assignment reporters dispatched from the newspaper office.

Overall, however, the courthouse reporter had one great ongoing resource. That was a kind of built-in voluntary system of reliable informants at virtually every level of courthouse business. These were news-wise officials, clerks, court attachés, attorneys, judges, deputy prosecutors, sheriff's deputies and others. Their information—tips—frequently relayed in courthouse corridors, were invaluable. It was a blessed practice that predated my time on the beat and for all I know is still the way of life.

One such incident, long etched in my memory, involved an attorney, his client (the defendant) and a Superior Court judge, all of whom would obviously have been pleased had a certain court action passed unnoticed by the press, as would likely have happened but for a court clerk who saw to it that it didn't.

It was approaching noon on a Saturday, the hour when virtually the entire courthouse was closed to the public for the weekend. Only one courtroom was open on Saturday mornings, mostly for the convenience of attorneys who had relatively minor legal papers to submit or matters of lesser importance to take up with the court. Such perfunctory Saturday court sessions were rarely worth a reporter's time.

The responsibility for presiding on Saturdays rotated among the many Superior judges. And on that day, the judge who presided was one of the least admired on the bench. He had been a little-known attorney with what newsmen and members of the bar considered lesser legal talent when the governor of the state made a surprise choice and named him to fill a vacancy on the bench. To some of us at the time, the question was how the governor found him, let alone singled him out for such recognition. Nevertheless, he filled his place on the bench, handling a calendar as busy as that of any other Superior judge. Interestingly, he sought to cultivate me and my friendship, likely thinking it a way to make an impression on the *Times*. Such approaches I politely accepted.

That late-hour Saturday hearing before him was the culmination of a long, much-deferred matter that had originated months earlier when a hit-and-run driver mortally wounded a pedestrian and sped away. It was a page-one story at the time. And days later, when police tracked down the damaged automobile and arrested the culprit, it was headline news, enhanced because the errant driver proved to be a scion of a well-to-do family of prominence.

He was charged and released on bail to await his day in court.

A long time elapsed as trial dates were set and continued. And the case faded from public attention.

Briefly, what occurred in the quiet of that courtroom was this. The defendant entered a plea of guilty, citing extenuating circumstances. His attorney asked for dismissal of the case. The defendant was set free.

It was minutes later when my informant sought me out and reported what had transpired.

By then the court was closed. The judge had departed. But the court reporter who had a verbatim record of the proceedings was still in the courthouse and willingly read it all to me: a necessity under the circumstances before I could move with the story.

The facts in the case were sufficient for page one in the Sunday editions.

But the crowning disillusionment was what I had seen and heard in that judge's own courtroom only a few days earlier. And I simply could not reconcile the two occurrences. At the end of the earlier trial, the judge almost literally threw the book at a young defendant, a husband and father, a stockbroker, who indeed was found guilty by a jury of appropriating clients' money. The amounts seemed less than enormous, perhaps a few hundred dollars here, a thousand or so there. He would certainly have to pay for the crime—temptations in a devastating depression period notwithstanding. But the penalty handed out by the judge seemed unrelenting—a series of consecutive terms, one for each offense, to be served in the state penitentiary for years to come. As he reeled them off, I wondered whether the judge distinguished between *consecutive* and *concurrent* since so many penalties levied by judges for gross crimes were made to run concurrently.

Covering that early trial, I can say that I felt compassion for the offender.

This was in mind when I called the city desk to relay the story of the now-free hit-and-run driver. My suggestion was that the present story make reference to the judge's decisions in the two cases.

But I lost. The city desk said "No." The second story ran on its own.

The courthouse was where I first became mildly aware of a young attorney who would enter politics and gain a place of distinction as a long-time nationally prominent senator from the state of Washington. His name: Warren G. Magnuson.

Our paths crossed in the courthouse, but like many tyros in the legal profession his cases then were decidedly more important to his clients than to newspaper readers. Ours was little more than a nodding acquaintanceship. In a second incarnation, it might be well to establish a cosy first-name relationship with every blossoming attorney with the thought that any one of them could become a senator. Or a President. If only you could tell which ones would make it!

The exploit of another young attorney, then in his early twenties, proved far more newsworthy and gained him ample pictures and publicity. His name was Alex Caplan. Like many new arrivals in the legal profession, he was yet to win his spurs on all counts except for wit and a rewarding sense of timing.

State and county elections were in the offing, and hopefuls were busily filing for offices.

On the last filing day, Caplan had his eye on the goings-on. Detecting that candidates had declared themselves for every judicial office but one, he appeared at the county clerk's offices just before closing, paid his filing fee and thus became the only candidate to enter the race for that position. In effect, he won the election before it was held.

It was perhaps easy enough for more experienced, more learned judges and candidates to overlook that one spot. It was for a short term of three months to fill a vacancy created by a retirement. The more seasoned candidates had their eyes on the long term and missed their opportunity to pull an "Alex Caplan."

We had known each other since high school days. So it was appropriate for Alex to seek me out to tell me of his coup, which opened the door to much newspaper attention for him.

There were stories following his elevation to the bench. Seasoned attorneys appeared before the black-robed young judge, and they may have quietly gulped but they addressed him as "Your Honor." The fledgling judge handled himself with appropriate decorum. His rulings were accepted.

Chapter 11

*Living in the Great
Depression*

Among all the ways that the history of the
Great Depression is recorded—including books, photographs, motion
pictures, periodicals, news stories, newsreels, letters, public records—
one of the more revealing is newspaper advertisements of the period,
which tell, among other things, how swiftly the economy was eroding.

Thus, a bare three months after the October 1929 stock market
crash that touched off the Depression, the housing market was wav-
ering, particularly in prices of medium-level homes whose owners—or
prospective buyers—were presumably at lower income levels. Real estate prices in the Northwest were always a notch or two below com-
parable property in older parts of the country and interest rates a notch
or two higher. But newspaper classified advertising columns began to
herald true bargains, such as $3,975 for a "lovely" brand-new five-room
home with attic in an attractive Seattle residential district. Or a furnished
bungalow, reduced to $2,850 with a down payment of $400. Or a
furnished home, including radio and Victrola, for $3,300.

Suddenly, jobholders were jobless. Unemployment was rising, and
prices on goods and services were falling.

No one could say whether Seattle was worse or better off than the
rest of the country. But one thing was surely certain: Seattle was not
very well off.

Within weeks after a mid-December 1929 headline story in the
Times reported that automobile prices were due to rise in 1930, the
industry clearly began to have second thoughts. Car manufacturers and
dealers unveiled heavy advertising campaigns, offering cars at bargain
prices, including many that were then familiar names but would pass

entirely from the scene. General Motors' Oakland V-8s, for instance: $1,120 delivered in Seattle. Or a four-door Essex sedan, built by Hudson (a name also destined to vanish) marked down to $765 from $1,030.

If you chose to travel to the Midwest to purchase your car FOB factory, the Oakland cost $1,045. A new Studebaker-8 of your choice, $1,285 to $1,765. Or a "new dynamic" Erskine, built by Studebaker: $875; a Chevrolet, depending on choice of models, $495 to $695, a Chrysler-6, $845. Or a Ford with "new roomy bodies, new smaller wheels, new larger tires and new colors": $435 and up.

Reflecting the times, Stutz Motors went into a collapse in December 1929, and its stock dropped to 1⅝ a share on the Curb Market (pre-American Exchange). In 1920, Stutz stock had sold for as high as $724 a share.

In February 1930, gasoline dropped a couple of cents a gallon to 19¢ as a price war opened in Seattle, and by July it cost variously 9 or 10 cents a gallon, or five gallons free with an oil change at some stations. Such prices prevailed in oil-rich southern California during Depression years but had never before been heard of in the Northwest. As price wars eased, gasoline sold for 20 to 21½ cents, and organized dealers in Seattle were striving to stabilize the price at 13 cents a gallon.

In February 1930, if your taste ran to music, you could drop in at the Seattle store of the well-known Pacific Coast musical instrument company, Sherman & Clay Company, and take your pick of 250 new grand pianos made by the Aeolean Company, Boston, for $455 each, payable on easy terms.

The well-known nationally advertised man's shoe, Florsheim, was priced at under $10 a pair, while one popular medium-quality men's clothing store, Lundquist Lilly, offered a pair of new "solid leather men's shoes" free to the purchaser of any two-pants suit or topcoat priced at $23 to $43. Frederick & Nelson, one of the class department stores, sold men's broadcloth shirts at $1.65 each, three for $4.50, and Irish linen handkerchiefs at 65 cents a dozen.

Full-page newspaper advertisements announced in October 1931 that "Hart Schaffner & Marx clothes are back to the prices of fifteen years ago."

Homemakers found food prices in chain stores similarly tempting: 5 cents a pound for navel oranges and bananas. Head lettuce, 5 cents. Seedless raisins, four pounds, 25 cents. Two pounds of California walnuts, 45 cents. Jap oranges, the popular import remembered from growing-up days, 85 cents per box containing four or five dozen. Winesap apples, four cents a pound or $1.59 for Northwest-size box. Prices on staples were correspondingly moderate.

And there were closeouts at high-quality clothing shops and other failed establishments, offering enormous bargains. The only hitch for many of us with jobs but declining incomes—it was rarely possible to splurge.

For anyone who did not experience it, the Depression might be thought of, somewhat mistakenly, as one dismally depressing day after another. (We who lived through it called it simply "the Depression." It took time and years of retrospection for it to take on its permanent designation, the *Great* Depression.)

Depending on your place on the economic scale, the readings ranged from sad—often desperate—for the poor and unemployed to not-too-badly-off for the middle ground to very much all right for the semi- and truly affluent. Notwithstanding progressive cuts in newspaper salaries, as in other businesses and enterprises—mine on its way down from a respectable $40 a week to an ultimate low of $28.75—my evaluation was that I, along with my colleagues, were in the not-too-badly-off middle range. We were working!

Working, yes. But there was little, if any, money for "frivolous" spending, such as dining occasionally at an upper-level restaurant or an evening out with a girl—even when dinner for two at choice restaurants barely touched $4 and top-of-the-line movie houses cost 50 cents. I recall how I lost the companionship of a girl—a delightful conversationalist, attractive and fun to be with—as I sensed I would, for no better reason than that I would be judged too chintzy. Here was I, a working newspaperman—and never buying her as much as a book, a bouquet or a modest dinner.

People who had to depend on aid of some kind found the going doubly difficult, especially in the earlier Depression years when relief was more improvised than planned, public welfare and private social agencies alike being unfailingly short of funds. In 1929 budget-making times, who foresaw the need to plan for hard times? After all, the collapse was precipitous and generally unexpected, coming on the tail of a period of euphoric prosperity.

In February and March 1930, sporadic rioting broke out when unemployed protest marchers formed in the Skidroad area for planned marches through downtown, only to be dispersed when police using nightsticks, sometimes mounted on horseback or riding motorcycles, bore down on them. This was similar to what was happening elsewhere in the country: protest marches and farmers' uprisings against foreclosures and low-low prices offered for their produce, among others. An Associated Press story from Cleveland reported how, in February 1930, between 1,000 and 2,000 unemployed men and women stormed City Hall only to be turned back by club-swinging police, with injuries to 20 of the crowd and 2 police officers. The story repeated itself around the nation.

Then-Mayor Frank Edwards angrily labeled "our" would-be marchers "Communists and radicals," names echoed by the police, and issued an ultimatum, reported in front-page newspaper stories on March 1, 1930: "Communists will not be permitted to make a hostile demonstration or uprising in Seattle on March 6 (a widely preannounced date for protest marches) or on any other day." Such confrontations were only a prelude to a far more dramatic demonstration three years later, reported in the following chapter.

It was ironic for Edwards, a mayor of uncertain popularity, that he was ousted from office the following year in an overwhelming recall vote on a totally unrelated matter. He had made a politically devastating, widely unpopular move in dismissing one of the city's most popular public servants, J. D. Ross, longtime city light and power superintendent. The new mayor, Robert H. Harlin, promptly reappointed Ross and also reshuffled the Police Department hierarchy, naming Detective Captain William B. Kent—another of my Police Department friends— to replace Police Chief Louis J. Forbes.

If personal experience may be a credible guideline, it can be said that deep depressions are *not* joyous times, but there were many joyous experiences (beyond those accumulated in the course of newspapering). That they were spun of very simple fabric made them no less pleasurable.

For instance, those occasional summertime nights when six or eight of us from the *Times* would drive to a saltwater beach north of the city for a moonlight dip in the altogether, a supply of beverages on hand to spark things up. Unfailingly, one valued member of the party was Ed (Edward J.) Kamm, an assistant city editor and first-rate newsman: a brawny man, 35ish, with bushy mustache, one of the merriest friends I ever had. It was a sad day for all of us on the *Times* when he was let go in a cutback. And infinitely sadder when, after moving to Salt Lake

City and joining the *Salt Lake Tribune,* he was fatally injured in a freak swimming accident, breaking his neck sliding down a toboggan chute.

And there was one New Year's Eve when four or five of us celebrated with an all-night poker party at the home of one of the group, enjoying good food, ample liquid refreshments, companionship and a moderately high-stakes game that ran until morning. It is likely that each of us had the protection of a guardian angel. No one would have reneged on his losses. But money was in tight supply for all of us. Fortunes shifted back and forth. But when the time came to settle, no one had won or lost more than 25 cents. A game to remember!

In late summer 1932, my elder brother Melvin drove to Seattle, traveling in his 1930 Ford roadster with rumble seat. By grace of his generosity and our always close fraternal relationship, the roadster was soon to be mine.

His trip came as an inspiration of the moment: in part to see me, in part to satisfy persistent nostalgia for the city that harbored many romantic memories for him—a city he loved—and in part for a change of pace from a play he was writing, which later would be produced on Broadway.

Soon, however, he felt an abiding urge to get back to his writing. Electing to cut the time it would take to drive, he presented his car to me and returned to New York by train.

Like the bicycle that gave me wings in my teen years, the little Ford—somewhat paint-weary but in impeccable mechanical condition—added a new dimension to life. Later, it would provide transportation when I too left Seattle for New York.

This was also the year in which I upgraded my living conditions, moving from a fairly simple, if reasonably comfortable, bachelor apartment at the fringes of downtown, where my monthly rent was $25, to one of the city's most elegant and fashionable apartment hotels, The Camlin, where I paid $20 a month.

Had it not been for financial pressure, I would likely never have been inspired even to think of negotiating such a transaction. My situation at the time can be appreciated by anyone who has tried juggling four or five balls while running to keep up with them as they edge away.

In my juggling act, the most important ball of all was the career that was developing so well. And no obstacle in the world was going to interfere with it. Not only were my editors reassuring, but I began to realize that opposition newspapers were now assigning their star, byline reporters to major stories I worked on: reporter-writers such as the *P.-I.*'s Hal Armstrong and Robert B. (Bob) Bermann, who cut such a figure with his neatly twirled mustache and sartorially correct grooming. It was a period when newspapers were far more sparing with bylines than they would become in later years—and though in *Times'* fashion I was only rarely accorded a byline, the feeling was good and reassuring.

In addition to other matters pressing for attention, including efforts to repay a student loan that had helped me through my senior year at the university, I was trying my best to hold onto two choice pieces of property remaining from the days of association with my father in real estate.

One was a 10-acre peach and apple orchard in Kennewick in fertile eastern Washington—later, in the Atomic Age, to become a power-rich high-prosperity area. This I finally lost for failure to pay taxes, a financial burden I could no longer carry while trying to manage the place from a distance of 200 miles, never receiving a nickel of income from the resident caretaker.

The other property was an old apartment building on a large and valuable lot in Seattle's Ballard District. Both my father and I foresaw a time when with a little prosperity the land, even sans building, would be worth considerable money, likely well into a six-figure range, representing a tidy profit.

I never discussed this with my parents, but my hope was to preserve it for them in their advancing years.

However, this too was lost when I could no longer keep up payments on the $2,500 mortgage—an amount that in later years would have been considered piffling but which in those days was a heavy burden. I just might have succeeded had the apartment tenants not been shrewder and more agile than I. Instead of paying their admittedly modest rents, they generally pleaded impoverishment (perhaps real), sometimes offered a few dollars as interim payment on their obligations, then moved in the dark of night after a free ride lasting a few months. There was no easy solution; it was plain that having the place occupied at least spared it from vandalism and deterioration. In any case, income was next to nil while the obligation fell to me to pay for gas and water, both provided. Plus taxes. Plus insurance. Plus regular payments to the hard-nosed mortgage holder.

Of course, I had no corner on tough luck. It was everywhere. It was the times.

And there stood The Camlin, the extravagantly conceived brain-child of two of the city's prominent financial figures, who had spared nothing in the lavish use of imported marble, elegant fixtures in baths, kitchens and elsewhere and regal appointments throughout. It was no secret that it was not paying its way. Nor would the men who brought it into being ever profit from it. Rather, both would face indictment, arrest and trial on grand larceny charges alleging misappropriation of funds from a failed savings and loan association that each had served as president.

After eyeing The Camlin—as it seemed to eye me—every time I departed and returned to the nearby Hampstead Arms apartment where I lived, I was moved to action. One day, I stopped to chat with the resident managers, an attractive young couple named McDonald. The establishment enjoyed a "name" and attracted name visitors and per-manent and semi-permanent residents who could afford it. The only problem: not enough of them.

The managers and I came to the point rather easily: what The Camlin lacked was a dash of dignified publicity to showcase the quality clientele that visited and lived there and to better establish its presence. We agreed that I should handle it. The McDonalds were impressed by my position on the *Times,* and we struck a deal. I would have one of their handsome suites at the token rent of $20 a month and provide publicity services, a responsibility that proved undemanding. The McDonalds and I were pleased with the results, and I enjoyed The Camlin as home for nearly two years before deciding to give up down-town living to move to the pleasant, invigorating atmosphere of the University District.

There, Floyd Flint, my longtime friend and university classmate of past years, and I shared an apartment just two short blocks from the campus: a happy interlude, made possible by my little Ford, which took me all the extra miles to and from work and elsewhere with the greatest of ease.

Floyd and I had met when we entered the School of Journalism, and our friendship matured and lasted over the years—even when we were separated by long distances—until his untimely death in 1968. From the outset, we found that our outlook and attitudes were highly compatible on much of life as we knew it: on politics, the social order, books, adventure, careers (though his interest was advertising, mine the editorial-writing side of newspapering) and girls—whom I approached with greater reserve while he, tall, articulate and assured, was much more the activist.

I think our friendship was sealed for all time when I learned that he shared my view on the election of 1928, when I cast my first and fruitless vote for President. My choice was Al Smith, the four-time Democratic governor of New York: my dominant conviction, above admiration for his progressivism and his opposition to prohibition—because he was a Catholic, and I believed it was past time for the electorate to bring the nation's religious prejudices to an end. Then and thereafter, we were both Democrats.

One thing to be said for the Depression—there was rarely a dull moment.

There was the time in the spring of 1931 when Nicholas Oeconomacas landed on page one of the *Times* with a half-pathetic, half-amusing solution to his torment of the moment: how to raise money to forestall his landlord's threat to turn him out of his home unless he paid his rent.

Oeconomacas was one of our best-known musicians, a featured member of the Seattle Symphony Orchestra for more than 20 years, considered one of the most gifted clarinetists in the Pacific Northwest. But he was out of work—a plight he claimed was shared by 200,000 professional musicians throughout the United States.

He determined to take his beloved clarinet to the streets to play for money. It was his last hope, he said. And the *Times* gave him a big sendoff with a story and a full-length picture showing him in the big black hat and full-length cape he affected, his clarinet to lips. The paper followed a few days later, as the street corner concerts were about to begin, with a complete list of times and places he would play.

The exploit was a success. The response was generous. Oeconomacas paid the rent.

If travel was on your mind during the years of the Depression, you had a choice of rare bargains. In early 1931, the Southern Pacific and the Union Pacific railroads introduced cent-a-mile rates between Portland, Oregon and the east. (Chicago, the terminus of the western lines, was "the east" to us.) Not to be outdone, the Chicago, Milwaukee, St.

Paul and Pacific led the way with a competitive cent-a-mile schedule between Seattle and the east.

And by May the *Times* carried a page-one story telling how "slashed railroad fares" would boost summer tourist traffic to Seattle. The round-trip fare between the Atlantic Coast and the Pacific Northwest: $125.

But travel by train was only one way to go.

For what was a lovely overnight trip by ship, the SS *Sol Duc* sailed regularly between Seattle and Bellingham, Washington, at the going rate of $1 each way. The *Sol Duc,* built for ocean travel but then plying the smooth waters of Puget Sound, left Seattle late each night. You did not have to buy a stateroom if you preferred to enjoy the lusty summer night breezes and short naps on deck, but for another dollar or two you could have a stateroom of your own.

That was a weekend trip I made a number of times, sometimes alone, sometimes with a companion. And on rare occasions when it was possible to arrange an added day off, we would take the mail boat out of Anacortes, a stop before Bellingham, and putt-putt through the beautiful San Juan Islands to the prize of them all—Orcas Island, where the family had its last Northwest land possession, 960 acres that stretched from warm-water Eastsound up Buck Mountain to a private 40-acre lake. (It was owned by the family, as distinguished from the two real estate holdings that belonged to me.) Fate was unkind. This elegant property was lost, too, as the Depression wore on, again for what seemed the jinx number of the times—a $2,500 mortgage that could not be paid. My father tried over a period of years before leaving Seattle to sell it for what he correctly termed and advertised it, "A Sportsman's Paradise." But even at the offered price of around $35,000 there were no takers. It was in 1975 when my wife and I made what was for me a sentimental journey to Orcas Island. There we learned that the property, which had passed from hand to hand, had been brought two years earlier for nearly $1 million. For what purpose? A tree farm—and a sportsman's paradise.

Measured in terms of economy, plus a dash of excitement, the least costly of all my Depression travels was the first in a succession of year-after-year summer vacation trips to Los Angeles, where I visited my parents and brother Davy, who then, as David Lewis, was a Hollywood motion picture producer.

The economy entered when City Editor Rudy Block quietly arranged a no-cost flight for me on a newly inaugurated Seattle–San Francisco airline. ("Quietly" because the *Times* had a sometimes-but-not-always-enforced rule against freebees for its employees.) The trip was made in a Ford Trimotor that left Seattle's Boeing Field about 9 A.M. and landed in the Bay Area eight hours later. The San Francisco–Los Angeles leg, via bus, was not a freebee. The trip back reversed the procedure.

What proved to be a one-of-a-kind vacation trip to California was via a newly introduced but short-lived way to travel: sleeper bus. The cost was roughly equivalent to train fare. But what elegance on a bus! At night the seats were converted into comfortable berths, just as on a Pullman car, a basin with running water at your elbow. There were restrooms and a galley that served meals. And all the requisite attendants. Happily for me and my fellow travelers, there were no more than three or four passengers aboard. Had the bus carried a full complement, space limitations would likely have made it much overcrowded. And that no doubt was reason enough for the failure of the double-deck sleeper bus as a new means of travel in the United States.

But what must have been the most spectacular bargain of all—for me and thousands of other summer travelers—was by ship, Seattle to Los Angeles, on either of two Alexander Line vessels, the swift and luxurious SS *H. F. Alexander,* which carried 560 passengers and made the round trip weekly, or the delightful—if a little slower and less capacious—SS *Ruth Alexander.*

I have long remembered the tempting Depression fare: $19.50 each way, including everything. A little less if you departed at San Francisco rather than traveling all the way to Los Angeles.

My friend Conny of the *P.-I.* and I traveled together on the *Ruth Alexander* on what for each of us was our first ocean trip. I remember one among many luxuries we discovered: calling the officer in charge by telephone after returning to our stateroom for the night and ordering sandwiches, all of course on the house, as were the gourmet meals served en route and the meticulous service throughout. And those handsome bulging trays of assorted sandwiches that arrived, embellished with salads and relishes that unfailingly included the largest plum-size ripe olives we had ever seen.

The next summer I repeated the trip alone, sailing on the *H. F. Alexander.*

Sadly, the *Ruth Alexander* was a World War II casualty, sunk on a wartime mission.

The *Seattle Times* generated news of its own in those years, some of it traceable to Depression pressures.

One, which set the paper on a course that its constituency never dreamed possible, came in January 1930, when publisher-owner C. B. Blethen announced in a page-one story and accompanying editorial that a 40 percent interest in the *Times* had been acquired by Ridder Brothers, New York publishers and owners of a network of newspapers. This gave the new minority shareholders a stake they would hold through the years. Blethen explained the move with a published statement to the effect that the complex duties and responsibilities involved in publishing a newspaper of the size and importance of the *Times* "had become too great for one man" and emphasized that "absolute control and management of the property will remain with him, and after him, with his family."

Five months later the *Times* announced that it was about to start construction of a greatly expanded new home for itself, out of the midtown area for the first time since it was established in 1896. Publication in the new quarters began in February 1931, and they were my base of operation, too, for a considerable part of my life with the *Times*.

What was unquestionably the most electric of all editorial shifts the *Times* could—and did—make came during the 1932 Presidential campaign, when the Great Depression was worsening week by week. *Anyone* who knew the *Times* knew that it never had to taste the bitter pill of supporting a Democratic candidate for any office or championing any Democratic position.

To sum it up briefly, the *Times* was—and so acclaimed itself— staunchly Republican.

Until.

On July 2, 1932, Govenor Franklin D. Roosevelt of New York was nominated for President on the Democratic ticket at the Chicago convention, with John N. Garner, Speaker of the House of Representatives, as his running mate. And then came Roosevelt's acceptance speech.

And on July 6, a *Times* front-page editorial appeared under the head

ACTION OF CONVENTION AND
ROOSEVELT LEADERSHIP WIN
THE TIMES TO HIS BANNER

"It was a speech from the heart of a sound American, coined into convincing words and phrases in the mind of one whose capacity for public service has been amply demonstrated," the editorial acclaimed.

"Read the speech; read it in the light of your own experience of conditions in this country today. Then you will understand why the *Seattle Times* is for Franklin D. Roosevelt for President of the United States."

Except for what followed, one might have considered that the new blood that came with the newspaper's new minority ownership had tempered its editorial policy.

Meanwhile, the paper dropped its editorial page masthead, which had acclaimed it "Independent in Business and Religion but Republican in Politics," for a new slogan, "An Independent Newspaper."

For a while thereafter, FDR and his family received highly favorable news coverage in the *Times,* both in content and in choice positioning on its pages, while President Herbert C. Hoover and his running mate Vice President Charles Curtis, once darlings of the paper, lost their prime positions.

Until, again, it was as though the *Times* started biting its tongue, editorially, for the self-induced "blunder" it had made. And within weeks, Hoover was once more the *Times'* darling and its clear choice for reelection.

No editorial disclaimer was needed but by October, as the campaign reached high heat, *anyone* who knew the *Times* knew that it did not want Roosevelt as President.

The news play was all in Hoover's court.

Thus, a page-one headline:

GOP TIDE IS RISING IN THE STATE
REPUBLICANS MAKE SUBSTANTIAL GAINS AFTER
SPEECHES BY HOOVER AND MILLS

And the story under it reported: "President Hoover's speech at Des Moines and the broadcast of Treasury Secretary Ogden L. Mills' California addresses last week turned the tide Hooverward in the State of Washington for the first time in this campaign. . . . "

A few days later, the full text of a speech by ex-President Calvin Coolidge in New York's Madison Square Garden citing the need for Hoover was carried by the *Times.* Coolidge was quoted in part: "No government has yet been devised that could make the people prosperous all the time." And he could forecast "Democratic raids on the Treasury."

When it was all over, a front-page editorial congratulated Roosevelt on his victory and went on to say: "If the *Times* does not at once join in the tumult of rejoicing over the victory won in the name of the

Democratic Party it is because, as a truly independent newspaper, the *Times* has too long held to its faith in the fixed principles of the Republican Party to be carried away by a shift in the breezes of public opinion. . . . "

The end of the third year of the Great Depression was accompanied by none-too-happy changes in the *Times* editorial staff. Bill (William D.) Chandler, who had opened the doors of the *Times* to me, had already resigned as managing editor to assume the same role for the *San Francisco Chronicle* when the second of two pillars of the *Times* editorial staff departed.

This, one of the most saddening changes of all as cutbacks continued, was the departure of City Editor Rudy Block.

Rudy had been a wise, gracious, cheerful leader of the reportorial staff during most of my time on the paper and for a long time before.

Enter his successor: Ray Felton, who had been the long-time managing editor of the *Seattle Star*. And the entire spirit of the editorial staff changed. It was as though a brisk Sousa march suddenly segued into Chopin's Funeral March without missing a beat: the consequences of an essentially nice guy in the wrong place at the wrong time with the wrong attitudes.

As will be seen later.

*J*ust 18 days before Franklin Roosevelt was inaugurated President, Seattle experienced the most ominous of all its Depression demonstrations. In light of history—the New Deal and a new day so near—it was an untimely hour for what many of us who were there feared might erupt into a deadly challenge to organized government.

This time it was not marchers and police confronting each other in a short, brawling encounter.

Interestingly enough, no one wanted a fight.

It simply evolved—almost spontaneously—into a contest and a 53-hour takeover of the seat of county government by demonstrator-members of the Unemployed Citizens' League. The League was formed in 1931 by jobless and down-and-outers and, as it grew by the thousands, gained recognition as their champion and spokesman.

I covered the story for the *Times* from beginning to end, aided and sometimes spelled by other reporters for snatches of rest. And when it was over, details fresh in mind, I wrote an article about it in response to expressed interest by the *New Republic*.

I have no recollection of ever having sent the manuscript to the magazine. Nor can I say how or why it landed instead in my personal files, there to remain until rediscovered long after the Seattle incident had passed. Perhaps the overwhelming excitement generated by the new Administration and its swift steps toward recovery simply diminished the significance of yesterday's events. In any case, it is unveiled here, just as written in February 1933: the anatomy of an explosive citizen demonstration.

They Took the Courthouse

Trailing behind a shabby little middle-aged drummer man, 2,000 organized men and women—some carrying placards and banners, some little children—marched down Seattle's Third Avenue and massed outside the King County Courthouse just before noon on February 14.

Protected by a police parade permit, they arrived to present demands to the County Board of Commissioners: they wanted gasoline and trucks for a pending state "hunger march" on the capitol at Olympia; they wanted cash doles and improvement in the county relief program.

In the end they received nothing except the satisfaction of having effected Seattle's boldest Depression demonstration during which they and some 3,500 reinforcements camped in the Courthouse for 53 hours, forcing King County's administrative government to suspend temporarily.

They moved into the Courthouse for a conference with the commissioners. For three days and two nights they remained, sleeping, eating, haranguing, talking, singing and operating the business of the extensive unemployed organizations. They piled into the commissioners' shiny public meeting room. They jammed the marble hallways, taking almost complete possession of one of the County-City Building's ten stories (above which is perched the new county jail). They flashed word by runners and telephone to unemployed throughout the city and county and used county telephones to call cities three hundred miles away. Crowds of new recruits poured in: men, women, children; whites and Negroes; clean and soiled; neatly dressed and tattered; shaved and whiskered; well and lame— all united by a perfect display of camaraderie.

They came in automobiles, street cars, afoot—and from outside the city in truckloads. They overflowed into City Hall Park.

The state unemployed chieftain, George E. Bradley of Bellingham, former railroad brakeman and erstwhile prosperous retail radio store proprietor, arrived. Orders were issued for a sympathetic state drive on Seattle. Unemployed from Spokane, Walla Walla, Everett, Bellingham, Tacoma, Olympia, Aberdeen and from adjacent towns and farms sent word they were coming. And they came.

They stayed until the evening of February 16 when 120 police and 30 sheriff's deputies peaceably evicted the demonstrators (while members of the National Guard assembled in Seattle's armory—a fact concealed in news accounts). City and county authorities anticipated bloodshed. All were surprised at the orderly evacuation.

When the 2,000 marched to the Courthouse none anticipated more than an afternoon's demonstration. The camping plan was conceived spontaneously. Somewhat irked because earlier in the day the director of the non-political King County Relief Commission refused to leave his uptown office to attend an outdoor mass conference where they could express their demands, the demonstrators went to the Courthouse intending to register their demands and depart.

After the crowd flocked inside the building, their calm, able young leader, William K. Dobbins, jobless laborer and father of three children, requested the two available county commissioners to appear before them. The third commissioner, Wilmer B. Brinton, was not present; he was before a jury in a Superior Courtroom upstairs, defending himself on a grand larceny indictment charging theft from the county—a charge of which he was later acquitted.

Commissioners John C. Stevenson and Louis Nash appeared. The crowd turned hopefully to Stevenson; they had helped elect him only three months ago. Through the massed cooperation of King County's 55,000 relief dependents he had received a substantial majority. They called him "John" and "Steve."

Amid whoops of approval from the ranks, Dobbins detailed the general demands: County aid for a March 1 drive to Olympia, three days work each week at $4.50 minimum wage, guaranteed doles of $10 for each single adult or family head and $3 for each dependent, "abolition of paid welfare workers hired to visit homes of the jobless and pass on eligibility" of relief recipients, repeal of a new state law embracing possible forced work clauses.

Commissioner Stevenson rejected support for the Olympia demonstration and explained he had nothing to do with the other demands. He told them to see King County's new $250-a-month welfare commissioner, William D. Shannon, a civil engineer who temporarily gave up his private business to direct relief activity.

That was the last straw. Shannon was the man who had refused to appear at a mass conference.

"They're giving us the run-around!" voices snapped. "Nobody will listen to us! There's no head to this relief thing at all! Get Shannon down here! Bring his whole board down here! We'll stay until Shannon and his board comes!"

Dobbins elbowed his way to the rostrum.

"You're running this," he told the crowd. "Do we stay here until Shannon and his board come?"

The crowd roared approval.

Had the relief commission come to the Courthouse for a conference at that time the demonstration would have ended. At that point the question was: Will the relief commission obey the conference ultimatum of the unemployed workers? The answer, No!

Throughout the 53-hour demonstration the slogan remained: "We'll stay until we get our demands!" The demands, however, developed in severity. The original ultimatum called for a conference with the relief commission—at the Courthouse. Then followed a demand that the commission appear and unconditionally agree to the program outlined by Leader Dobbins. On the second day of occupation the crowd resolved that Washington's Governor Clarence D. Martin must dissolve the Shannon relief commission, replacing it with appointees from the ranks of the demonstrators. On the third day they dispatched a message to the governor demanding he appear immediately before them.

Direction of the demonstration lay in the hands of the Committee of Twenty, previously elected from the membership of the Unemployed Citizens' League. The 2,000 marchers were U.C.L. members, Dobbins their president. But neither the Committee of Twenty nor President Dobbins bound the crowd to a single decision or promise or held a single discussion with Commissioners Stevenson or Nash without reporting to the swelling ranks and obtaining their approval—or disapproval.

Organizing for an indefinite stay, the Committee of Twenty dispatched self-styled "chiseling committees" throughout the city to forage food from restaurants, grocers, bakers, meat and fish dealers. The first evening the chiselers brought back meat and bread. The county jail superintendent, under orders of Commissioner Nash, sent pots of coffee and bread and meat. Everybody ate.

The following days the chiseling committees improved in efficiency: one group brought in a half beef, another a thousand pounds of fish, others crates of vegetables. A kitchen in the building was turned over to them.

City police patrolled the Courthouse for three or four hours the first evening until Seattle's Mayor John F. Dore ordered them away. (Mayor Dore and Commissioner Stevenson are political enemies. Conducting a noisy radio campaign, the mayor fought Stevenson's election, predicting bloody battles in Seattle if "that representative of the unemployed" were elected. There had been no bloody battles. But this was an ominous time.)

Demonstration leaders pleaded that there be no disorder. Dobbins appointed a policing force from the ranks, members being distinguished by white rags around one arm or six inches of red and black typewriter ribbon in their lapels. He declared the demonstration was no radical movement, that only an unimportant, negligible number of communists were in the crowd. He pleaded that every man and woman guard against provocateurs. That police force patrolled the hallways, stood at every doorway and permitted no one to enter the overcrowded chamber without credentials—notes signed by a member of the Committee of Twenty.

Through the night speakers aired grievances. Men and women sat on benches or lay on floors and slept. Delegations from other cities started massing in numbers.

The third day citizens throughout Seattle were becoming restive at the long siege. Businessmen were apprehensive. County and city officials saw no sign of abatement in the demonstration. Covert conferences were called—attended by businessmen, relief workers, the mayor, the county commissioners.

Returning from such an uptown conference, Commissioner Stevenson appeared before the demonstrators at noon of the third day. He issued a statement. He sympathized with the demonstrators, he said, but their job was done. He ordered them to leave the building by 5 o'clock. Surprised that Steve would say so, the crowd booed him. Hecklers threatened recall. He didn't give a damn, Stevenson replied. He wanted a peaceful evacuation, but warned that the sheriff was massing his deputies.

Robert Gordon, smiling young Negro secretary of the U.C.L., leaped to the rostrum amid cheers.

"Do we go or stay?" he demanded.

"Stay!" howled the crowd.

"That's not loud enough," he laughed. "Do you mean it?"

The crowd whooped, hurrahed, thundered, "Yes!"

More speeches. More truckloads from out of town. More reports from the chiseling committees. More shouts: "We stay until we get our demands!"

Meanwhile, Sheriff Claude G. Bannick called in deputies from outlying districts, National Guardsmen got ready machine guns at the armory, Stevenson asked Mayor Dore for support and the mayor agreed, calling uniformed men from beats, ordering city firemen to remain in reserve.

As the 5 o'clock deadline neared, the Courthouse was tense. Published reports of the eviction order attracted thousands of spectators outside the building. At 4:45 o'clock Dobbins requested another vote. The crowd shouted it would stay. Dobbins appealed, then, for no violence; requested passive resistance.

"Don't fight the bulls," he yelled. "Make them carry you out."

"We'll stay!" the crowd shouted when another vote was taken at 5 o'clock.

Five, ten, fifteen minutes passed. No one knew what was coming. At 5:20 o'clock, sheriff's deputies, wearing badges on their lapels, and uniformed police walked into the choked second floor corridor. They were smiling; that was their armor.

"You'll have to go," they informed the crowds in the hallways. And the crowds went, singing "Solidarity Forever." The deputies and police cleared the corridors and chambers. They laughed with the demonstrators, exchanged wisecracks, commended them for a brave stand—but firmly shoved unwilling evacuees out the doors. Licked, the demonstrators smiled, sang: "Solidarity forever, solidarity forever, solidarity forever, for the union makes us strong." Four men were arrested, released a few hours later without trial. A few were scuffed and bruised.

As an anti-climax, 1,500 men tried to re-enter the building. Police at the doorway strained against them. A firehose was turned on from an upper floor. The mob dispersed, organized in parade formation, marched through downtown streets.

Hundreds piled onto street cars paying no fare, calling, "Charge it to Mayor Dore!" They rode free. Out of towners started home. The county contributed 150 gallons of gasoline to hasten the retreat.

Next day, Mayor Dore ordered a police guard around the County City Building, declared he will permit no more mass demonstrations or parades and will bar delegations of out-of-town demonstrators from the city. The next day, also, the Committee of Twenty, Dobbins and State Leader Bradley met, formulated plans for the March 1 drive on Olympia, decided to mass several thousand state unemployed in Seattle February 28.

Chapter 13

Changing Times

*I*t was the year for new names, new faces and *change* on the political scene.

And in our corner of the country, many who chose to wear the proper party label—which in 1932 meant Democratic—made it with relative ease.

How much they were aided, individually and collectively, by Franklin Roosevelt's landslide victory, how much by the voters' eagerness for change, how much by simply being judged the best men for the jobs did not much matter.

The point was that they were in, and they were new.

Among them were four who were known to me either casually or well.

There was Marion A. Zioncheck, who won a seat in the U.S. House of Representatives. I had known him as a fellow student at the University of Washington: a maverick who had achieved the "impossible" in being elected president of the student body, recognized as the only non-Greek-letter-fraternity man to make it in the highly charged fraternity-sorority climate. He was no sooner elected to Congress than the *Seattle Times* labeled him editorially as one of the "cuckoo candidates foisted on the people by the radicals."

There was Victor A. Meyers, elected lieutenant governor of the state. The *Times*, not too happy with the choice (he won over a "name" Republican), had itself transformed him only a year earlier from a locally known leader of a jazz band to a viable candidate for mayor of Seattle in a pure gag campaign. Dubbed the "personality candidate," who espoused such causes as a hostess on every streetcar and cracked ice on all "owl" streetcars at night, he cashed in on the attention he had earlier received in the mayoral campaign to win the lieutenant governor's race.

Doug Welch, one of our brightest writers and resident wit, had been assigned to direct and cover Vic Meyers' campaign for mayor. Welch needed little help in developing campaign gags, but the city desk and other reporters gladly did their part to keep things going. I remember one time when Doug returned to the editorial rooms to write his story for the day. A tall, ample man, he was garbed in a white sheet that barely covered his gartered sox. That was the day he and Meyers had simulated Mahatma Gandhi on a round of public appearances. The candidate also wore a sheet and had a white goat in tow.

And there were Charles H. (Dick) Todd, a fellow *Times* reporter, and Warren G. Magnuson, the young attorney whose path and mine had crossed in my courthouse days.

About three months before the election, the *Times* ran a news-feature story embellished with a four-column photograph featuring Todd, Magnuson and three other young men who had declared their candidacies in the approaching elections. Todd, a tall, spare chap who spoke in measured speech, was my successor on the police beat and became a warm friend.

The *Times* story referred to the candidates as "young sons of prominent families who would have been cotillion leaders in their fathers' day."

Cotillion leaders or not, Todd and Magnuson won their races for the state legislature on the Democratic ticket. Later, Magnuson rose to higher political levels, going on to serve for many years as a prominent progressive leader in the U.S. Senate. Todd, who served two terms in the state senate and one in the lower house, would recount in later years how he considered it one of his prime missions as a freshman senator to vote for repeal of prohibition, which he did, and which the legislature did. Having acquired a law degree en route, he resigned from the legislature midway through his third term to accept a post as an enforcement attorney for one of the federal agencies of the period, the Office of Price Administration (OPA).

Later still he would become legal counsel to the *Seattle Times*—quite a step beyond police reporter—and a long-time member and secretary of its board of directors.

On his thirteenth day in office, President Roosevelt sent a 72-word message to Congress urging immediate modification of the Volstead Act to permit the manufacture and sale of beer and other beverages whose alcoholic content would be permissible under the 18th Amendment to the Constitution. He urged it as a means of providing much-needed new taxes.

Congress acted with such speed that legislation legalizing 3.2 beer was enacted and the President signed the bill into law in less than two weeks. It also provided a beer tax of $5 per barrel and imposed a tax of $1,000 on manufacturers of the brew.

The effective date was April 7. The state legislature having passed enabling legislation—Washington was one of 19 states in the Union to be so forehanded—we on the *Times* were ready for it.

The day beer flowed was a smashing news day on the paper—though a dry one in the editorial rooms. I was named beer editor, and I can say that we turned out stories to warm the hearts of beer lovers, bankers and businessmen. Everything from the historic beginnings of beer making and beer drinking back to the early Egyptian brew that I remember from my research that day as *heqa* . . . to the revival of our local breweries and glass bottling manufacturing plants . . . to new life in the shipping business . . . to how and where to buy beer . . . to the promise of resurgent prosperity . . . and most everything in between. Before the end of 1933, the entire prohibition era passed into history.

As the *New York Times* told it with precision on page one on December 5, 1933: Prohibition would pass into history as an unsuccessful experiment the next day—13 years, 10 months, 18 days and a few hours after it was declared in effect. By that time, conventions in the states of Pennsylvania, Ohio and Utah would have ratified the 21st Amendment to the Constitution.

It would be a long time before the Great Depression ended. Depending on what part of the nation you were monitoring—New York, for instance—it would take longer. I sensed an easing of the crunch in Seattle by mid-1934. By mid-1934 also, I was soon to learn, parts of West Texas were bursting with job-abundant prosperity.

What the new Administration did from the moment of its inception, however, was to lift the spirits of the people. Something was being done to stop the Great Slide and to start rebuilding. It was felt in our Northwest country. There was no upward movement in *Times* salaries; they continued at their lowest Depression levels. But at least it was possible to anticipate improvement.

It was refreshing to see headlines appear such as this one, from the March 16, 1933, *Seattle Times,* for the first time in three years:

STOCKS UP 8.26 POINTS

And three days later, following the historic General Bank Holiday declared by the President almost immediately after taking office:

BIG INCREASE IN RETAIL SALES

REOPENING OF BANKS
STIMULATES BUSINESS

If it was a moment of euphoria for the country at large, it was something else, however, for the microcosm that was the editorial department of the *Seattle Times*. It was unmistakably a time of change—change that was visited on us with the arrival of our new city editor, Ray Felton. Had he come in with a more benign appreciation of human relations and tolerance for the opinions and sensibilities of those who worked under him, my story and the stories of several colleagues could well have turned out very differently. But that was not the way things went.

In appearance and demeanor, Ray could have been a stern, old-time schoolmaster in shirtsleeves with a tendency to peer over his glasses when expressing himself. It was hard to believe that he was lacking in humor, but I cannot remember one instance when he displayed it in dealing with me or other reporters.

It was unlike the old days, when a sense of camaraderie had prevailed between reporters and writers and the city desk . . . when City Editor Rudy Block and his assistants would encourage creativity on the part of reporters and would find opportunities—as did Managing Editor Bill Chandler—to praise jobs well done.

The atmosphere now was chilly. Reporters found less pleasure in their work. And their once-exhilarating creativity washed away.

It was a repeated wrench for those of us to whom it happened to deliver significant stories—even scoops—into Ray's hands only to see him read and tuck the copy into his desk drawer, often to remain there unless an opposition newspaper chanced to publish a story on the same subject. Then chances were that the *Times* would follow with a cutdown version, bringing up the rear when it could have blazed the trail.

Such was his long-lasting impact that, decades later, newsmen who had worked on the *Times* during his administration would recall their distaste for the experience on all counts but one. Had it not been for him, they could reflect, many who had left the paper rather than continue under the circumstances might well not have achieved the success they did in other surroundings.

And the *Seattle Times* was the point of origin for many personal success stories.

Chapter 14

The End and a
New Beginning

I have never forgotten the day Fred Lynch was fired. Nor the seriocomic interplay between him and City Editor Ray Felton.

Fred, about my age, was a highly competent reporter, a bright and witty writer, dark haired, pleasantly good looking, who had the makings of a bon vivant.

It so happened that his desk and mine faced each other, both near the city desk, which—though I would gladly have foregone it—gave me a front row seat for the action that took place.

It was a morning in late 1933 or early 1934 when Fred made his appearance in the editorial rooms a long hour past the prescribed 8 o'clock starting time. Without taking off his topcoat or hat, he sat at his desk, rolled a sheet of copy paper into his typewriter and began to hammer away as though rushing to write the hottest story of the week with only moments to go before deadline; in reality, the next deadline was more than an hour away.

In a moment or two Felton was at his side, demanding to know where he had been.

Not to be interrupted in his purposeful operations, Fred continued to type, neither answering nor looking up.

Felton's short fuse was beginning to burn, and he demanded: "Why were you late?" It became clear that Fred had received earlier warnings to get to work on time. But he made no response as his fingers pounded the keys.

In obvious exasperation, Ray blurted: "You're fired! Get out!"

Rising from his chair, Fred pulled the copy paper from the type-writer, stuck it into a pocket and with a full display of dignity strode from the room.

That closed out the relationship between the *Times* and Fred Lynch: a loss to the newspaper, a gain for him.

It was not long after his departure that word came back from him in New York. Soon after arriving there, directly from Seattle, he had landed an executive-level position with the Radio City Music Hall, an association he would enjoy for years. Still later came word that he had married a dancer he met there, a Radio City Music Hall rockette.

What his colleagues on the *Times* well knew was Fred's value as a newsman, and one of their memories was how only a couple of years before his dismissal he had played a minor hero's role covering the last hours of the Great Schooner Race of the winter of 1931.

The Great Schooner Race preceded Felton's arrival. It was one of the last achievements of the kind by the spirited, highly professional city desk crew—soon to be displaced—that I knew from my earliest days on the paper.

What the desk did was to turn the sailing of two Seattle-bound windjammers from Hawaii into a race that had readers of the *Times* and of newspapers across the country edgy with anticipation for a full month. It was in the same league as various other news-making ploys of *Times* invention, such as the mayoral campaign of Jazzman Vic Meyers, the "personality candidate."

Some of us on the paper who saw it unfold were certain at the outset that the "race" was no race at all. But you did not have to be a believer to applaud the ingenuity of the feat.

It began in late November when the four-masted schooner *Commodore* sailed from Honolulu. Six days later, the five-masted schooner *Vigilant* left the same port. Both were returning in ballast. It was likely, if unconfirmed, that our quiet, good-humored marine editor, R. H. "Skipper" Calkins, shared his reports of the two departures with the city desk and thereupon the race was hatched among editors.

Both ship captains were known for their sense of humor, as could have been affirmed by Skipper Calkins, a veteran of long years in his field. It would take little more than an exchange of messages with, and between, them to make a race of it. In any case, the captains soon were well into the spirit of the venture.

There followed a continuing stream of stories in the *Times* and, via wire services, in many other newspapers recounting all the cliff-hanging details of the race, the effects of storms at sea, the ships' progress and setbacks—even exchanges between the two captains. A few days out of Honolulu, for instance, just before his radio mysteriously went silent, to remain that way for days, *Vigilant* Captain Charles Mellburg wirelessed a challenge to his counterpart, *Commodore* Captain B. N. A. Krantz, wagering that his ship would win. The captain of the *Commodore* not only accepted the bet but raised the stakes.

Ordinarily, the 2,200-mile voyage took 20 days. But unusually heavy weather slowed the progress of both ships. Which only heightened tensions.

So it went until a few days before Christmas, when the tug *Golliah* put out from Seattle to meet and tow the winner to port. And this was where Fred Lynch entered the scene, accompanied, as I recall, by our doughty photographer Smitty, both of them sailing on the tug to cover the closing days of the event. Thereafter, the pages of the *Times* were enlivened by Fred's stories and a series of sensational photographs, including shots of the winner shown half buried in the high seas.

The first of Fred's dispatches, December 23, appeared under the page-one banner headline "COMMODORE WINS SCHOONER RACE," reporting how the *Golliah* reached the ship in heavy seas 35 miles off Cape Flattery and took her in tow: the *Commodore,* "riding the swells of the Pacific as gracefully as a huge white bird," was declared winner. And lashed to her foremast, the ship's broom, symbolic of victory in the ocean routes.

Then a brief note reporting on the vanquished: "The five-masted *Vigilant,* hopelessly beaten in the contest, was only 870 miles from Honolulu at 2 o'clock this morning and approximately 1,400 miles behind her four-masted rival."

The race was over, but thanks to the presence of Fred Lynch and our photographer, who saw it all from the deck of the *Golliah,* the dramatics had a considerable way to go.

The day after the *Commodore* was taken in tow, the lines parted in a storm, inspiring a page-one *Times* headline: "RACE SCHOONER ADRIFT IN GALES." That brought a relief ship to the scene, the historic *Roosevelt,* the ship that carried Admiral Robert E. Perry on his North Pole discovery voyage.

As though one crisis at a time was not enough, the next dispatch reported that the *Roosevelt* itself was believed lost at sea. . .

. . . until Christmas Day arrived and all was well. Our correspondent, fighting an unremittingly violent case of seasickness, as he had for days without revealing it in his dispatches, reported how the *Roosevelt* steamed into the calm waters of Neah Bay at dawn. It was safe, the *Commodore* was safe and so was the *Golliah*.

It was only days after Fred Lynch's dismissal that Felton took aim and lowered the boom on me. He needed a man to cover the police beat, and with no more than a command reassigned me to the job, adding what struck me as a double insult. He expected me thereafter to report to the police press room at 6 o'clock each morning—an hour earlier than ever.

I accepted the assignment, telling myself it was only temporary, knowing it was the beginning of the end of my relationship with the *Times*.

When I had joined the paper in 1929, I made a pledge to myself: in 10 years I would either be city editor or I would resign. (I never went as far as even to think of giving up my newspaper career. That was to be my lifetime pursuit.)

Now it was 1934. Starting my march backward, thanks to Ray Felton, I knew at once the course I would take. My paid vacation was less than six months away. I would hold out until then. After that, off to New York.

A month or two before takeoff, I shared my secret with Floyd Flint, my friend and apartment mate, and with my parents.

A few days before the appointed day, I ran into Oliver Morris, city editor of the *Post-Intelligencer,* told him I was leaving the *Times* and Seattle. He asked how he could reach me if he ever wanted to send greetings, and I gave him my parents' address in Los Angeles.

The day before packing my little Ford to drive to Los Angeles for a short visit with my parents, then on to New York, I said goodbye to the *Times*.

Next day: off for a new beginning.

A day or two before leaving Los Angeles for New York I received a telegram from Oliver Morris offering me a post with the *P.-I.* Not wanting it to happen, but fearing it might, I was prepared. By then I simply did not want to return to Seattle. Wiring him a reply, I boldly set my minimum salary at nearly four times my closing salary at the *Times*. His response: Come along. We'll meet it as soon as possible. Which was enough for me. I wired my regrets—and two days later headed east.

About eight months after arriving in New York I received a note from Oliver Morris telling me my *Seattle Star* colleague, Ross Cunningham, had joined the *P.-I.* staff and added: "You would probably be over here by now if you had remained in Seattle."

---

Chapter 15

*A*fter Seattle, I entered a whole new world, and life would never be the same. What happened . . . and how dreams long held can gradually melt away in a flood of unforeseen events . . . is told in the episodes and adventures that bring this story to a close.

On the Road

It was a little after mid-June 1934 when I drove out of Los Angeles bound for New York. Happily—and that is precisely the word—it was before the advent of freeways, thruways, expressways and other high-speed highways that cut time and miles by skirting, or totally avoiding, towns, cities and too much of the picturesque countryside. Otherwise I would have missed one experience after another that confirmed how good a time and how good a way it was to cross the country. Holbrook, Arizona; Odessa and Denton, Texas; Gettysburg, among others, became more than names to me.

Six hundred miles on the way, I pulled into a gasoline station in Holbrook, then a town of possibly 1,200. I barely had time to step out of the car when a neatly dressed man, perhaps a business or professional man, approached with a "good morning," then a question. Was I a physician? He said the town was in desperate need of a resident doctor; townspeople had put up money and were prepared to underwrite a doctor's expenses in setting up and getting under way.

Surely a tempting offer—for a doctor. I expressed warm thanks for being considered even momentarily.

Driving away, I decided I had experienced a small sign that the Depression was lifting, just as I had thought it seemed to be during my last weeks in Seattle.

It was in West Texas that I encountered a totally new experience: genuine, authentic, bona fide prosperity. New oil fields had been discovered, and Odessa was at the heart of the action.

Having driven more than 100 miles in the gathering dusk and evening light in a vain effort to find overnight accomodations in oil-fever country, I made a beeline on reaching Odessa for what in those days was one of the likeliest sources of tourist information: a gasoline station.

Holbrook had been a mere prelude to what was to unfold in Odessa. The gas station was alive with men dressed variously in Levis and overalls and sporting Southwest hats. A couple of them came over to me before I could get out of the car: on-the-spot job recruiters offering jobs-jobs-jobs. (Was I a welder? A pipe fitter? Interested in a job as a roustabout?)

One told me he was a school teacher from another part of Texas who had quit his teaching job midstream to get in on the Odessa excitement. He recounted how the town had experienced a false oil boom a few years earlier, when the population rose from virtually nothing to 2,400. Then the boom collapsed and almost everyone left. This was the real thing.

Commercial buildings on the main street, which had been only partly finished and abandoned in those earlier days, were being rushed to completion—not only for use as stores but as living accommodations for the people sweeping into town. He estimated that within the week past, the population had topped 2,000 and was growing by the day, if not the hour. Odessa's population in the 1980 census stood at 90,027.

But what about accommodations for the night?

We had established an amiable enough relationship that he felt he could suggest a tourist cabin on a back street (motels were yet to be invented), where I found clean, comfortable quarters for the night.

The next morning I explored the town and found it crowded and busy everywhere. Still the firehorse, I stopped at the local newspaper for conversation with the editor. He authenticated everything I had learned the night before. Hearing about my newspaper background, he held out a proposition to me. Perhaps I would be interested in buying the paper?

But, of course, even had I the money to buy it, nothing would have diverted me from New York and the newspaper career I dreamed of there.

I was off on the road again, surer than ever that the Depression was lifting.

There was Denton, Texas, where I spent a night in a tourist cabin. I remember the brilliant full moon, the cicadas chirping, a feeling of romance in the air. And walking into the main part of town, I knew that I had never seen as many beautiful unescorted girls and young women in one place. A rich temptation. Before leaving the next morning, I had the answer. Denton was the home of Texas Women's University, a large all-female school.

And there was a late Sunday afternoon on a crowded highway west of St. Louis, when a tragic accident stopped all traffic. A car, which I was to learn carried several members of one family, had gone off the road into a ditch. It burst into flames and no one inside was saved. There it was before my eyes—too much to restrain myself. I hurriedly went to work getting the story into focus, talking to witnesses—even managing to get names of some of the victims from a traveler who knew them.

I thought momentarily of finding a telephone and relaying the story to one of the St. Louis newspapers; then, in a flash it occurred to me: What the hell am I doing! Fortunately, a reporter from the *St. Louis Globe Democrat* appeared—a newsman usually can be spotted. I turned my collected facts over to him, got back into my car and as traffic moved continued driving east.

Before leaving Seattle I had written to my old police-beat colleague and friend, Conny Connaughton, continuing our sporadic correspondence. He had long before left the *P.-I.* and the West to return to his hometown, Wapakoneta, Ohio, and now was itching to go back to New York, where he had once lived and worked. It was agreed that I would stop in "Wapak," as the natives affectionately called it, pick him up and we would travel east together.

It turned into a pleasurable, leisurely interlude for both of us, heightened by a memorable spur-of-the-moment decision as we drove into Gettysburg in the late afternoon of the Fourth of July: we would visit the National Cemetery.

Our slow walk through the marked battle sites where nearly 50,000 Union and Confederate soldiers had perished just 71 years earlier, the seemingly endless graves, the grassy rolling terrain, is still a wistful memory for me. The sun would not set for another hour. The sky was an unblemished deep blue. We felt a mingled sense of patriotism and history. We were alone. Whatever crowds the earlier part of the day might have brought were gone.

Presently, a far-away sound filtered in, barely interrupting the still of the fading day. It was the hum of a reaper on a distant farm. It was an affecting moment. We paused, then turned and walked away, sad-happy as we resumed our travels and talked of that fragmentary experience.

A day or two later as we approached New York, I felt ready to slay the dragon.

Arriving there, Conny and I parted to seek our separate fortunes. We would meet again now and then over the years.

New York I

On my arrival, I was spared two problems: one, where to live; two, what to do with my automobile. My brother Melvin and his wife, Peggy, were spending the summer on their unfarmed farm overlooking the Delaware River in Bucks County, Pennsylvania, and made their Manhattan apartment on East 15th Street available to me. As for the car, I soon learned that it was both legal and safe to park on city streets day and night, just as at that time it was in the West. The American scene was not yet blessed with the ubiquitous parking meters of today, nor with the universal limited- and restricted-parking zones. There was even daytime parking on both sides of Fifth Avenue. New York's transportation being so available and cheap, I made use of it and left the car on the street.

I quickly settled in, and the long-planned pursuit of a career in a new setting began. And my first unsettling discovery was that West Texas was no bellwether.

New York was in a deep depression. I recall no street-corner apple sellers—a hallmark of early Depression days—though they may have been there. However, one never-forgotten telltale sign was the pushcarts spotted curbside along such heavily foot-traveled streets as 14th and 23rd: all piled high with half-pound Hershey and Nestle candy bars priced at a top of 10 cents each, sometimes a bargain-rate 9 cents.

But the severest blow came as I learned about available newspaper jobs. Practically speaking, there weren't any.

While dreaming of New York from a distance of 3,000 miles, I had no conception of the depressed state of the newspaper business there—nor of the entire publishing industry. (I have decided a hundred times since that my decision would have been the same had I known.)

The city was awash with qualified newspaper people, newpapering never having recovered from the death of the *New York World* in February 1931. The failure of that enormously prestigious paper meant that most of the 2,800 men and women who worked on the *Morning,* the *Evening* and the *Sunday World* were suddenly out of work. As the *New Republic* recounted in a sober obituary on March 11, 1931, it was a double blow, coming "at a time when there are already thousands of competent journalists walking the streets of New York."

It was easy enough to recognize a setback, but the pangs, fortunately, would soften.

Thanks to several very special people I was yet to meet: people who considered my newspaper background, education and attitudes right for a field they knew very well—even if I didn't—I was steered into public relations for social work.

The easing into it began on the day I determined to meet Paul U. Kellogg, editor of *Survey* magazine. It may be recalled that he and I had exchanged letters in my closing days at the University. And those were among the prize possessions I had packed for my cross-country venture. Before walking to the *Survey* offices on East 19th Street, I slipped them into a pocket.

I knew very well that it was chancy not to call ahead to ask for an appointment, but figuring the odds, decided against it. Entering his outer offices, I introduced myself to his secretary, told her I was newly arrived from Seattle and asked for a very few minutes with Mr. Kellogg. Noting her understandable reluctance, I handed her an envelope containing a copy of my letter to him and his reply and suggested that he might like to look into it.

Fortune was on my side. A brief wait and Mr. Kellogg stepped out, extended his hand and spoke the words I never have forgotten: "I have always wanted to meet the man who wrote that letter." Mr. Kellogg and I became friends (as did others I would meet through him), but I never had the courage to ask whether he *really* had remembered that five-year-old correspondence or was simply being totally gracious.

We spent more time in his office than I had expected. He was a soft-spoken man, older, of course, than I, penetrating but gentle in drawing me out. He felt I should meet two of his newspaper friends, Arthur Hays Sulzberger, who was then or about to be the newly named publisher of the *New York Times,* and J. David Stern, publisher of the *New York Post.* He called them in my presence and set up appointments for me. As editor of the principal magazine focusing on social work, he knew and suggested that I meet various social work notables, among them Mary Swain Routzahn, director of the Department of Social Work Interpretation of the Russell Sage Foundation, who would become an important figure in my nascent career. Mr. Kellogg assured me that I would be hearing from him and I departed.

The meetings with Mr. Sulzberger and Mr. Stern took me into the inner sanctums of their newspapers but led to no more than a few minutes' conversation with each. Meeting for the first time with Mrs. Routzahn, I found her warmly encouraging about prospects. She saw to it that I registered with the single most important placement agency in the field, the Joint Vocational Service, which was supported by the Russell Sage Foundation and the source to which social agencies throughout the country turned when seeking personnel. Mrs. Routzahn, too, assured me I would hear from her.

Later in the summer, I received a call from Helen Hall, headworker of the famed Henry Street Settlement (founded by the equally famed Lillian D. Wald) on New York's Lower East Side. Miss Hall was a friend—later to be the wife—of Paul Kellogg.

She extended me an invitation to live at the Settlement and undertake, if I would, some special writing on its behalf. It was an offer much like those extended over the years to a limited number of writers, artists and others in varied creative pursuits who rose to fame based on work performed at the Settlement.

Reassured by friends, old and new, that it was a prestigious relationship, I gladly accepted and lived for months in a part of Manhattan best known for its poverty, pushcarts and first-generation immigrants.

It was a totally new life for me, immersed in a part of the immigrant world I had barely been aware of. Although a bit edgy at first, I soon came to embrace that world.

Living was comfortable, including room maid service. There was always pleasant dining at a table set for 10 or 12, presided over by comely and gracious Miss Helen Hall and attended by two delightful young serving maids, Peggy and Molly, from Ireland. There was frequent ethnic dancing, in a sizable room just short of being a ballroom, that brought together immigrant-family neighbors who had come from various European countries.

I soon developed warm friendships. Among them, Joe Kelley, who was involved with the consumer protection movement; H. Stratton Price, a splended raconteur and good companion who spoke with a pronounced British accent; and a talented young painter named Day, who elected to paint my portrait, charging a fee of $15 which, at the time, was a considerable sum for me to muster. But I made it. The painting still hangs in our home.

I wrote various feature articles on behalf of causes championed by the Settlement: for example, pushing for lower milk prices to enable the poor to afford to drink it—*not* the higher prices voted by the state legislature to fund a drink-more-milk campaign on behalf of dairy interests. I had a rare opportunity, too, to meet key media people—one being Margaret Cuthbert, who headed the National Broadcasting Company's public service department. This grew into a long and fruitful relationship.

There was time as well for my own writing, and having two prized possessions with me—my portable typewriter and equally portable dictionary—began to plot out and write scripts for a dreamed-up radio series. Not unexpectedly, the theme centered on adventures in newspapering, but with a switch from what might have been more customary casting. My protagonist was a bright, brave, canny newspaperwoman named Marian Foster, coined from the names of two good newspaper friends in Seattle, Marian Badcon, my *Times* colleague, and Mike (Michael) Foster, an almost-fictional reporter on the *P.-I.* who would blossom into a fairly successful novelist.

It never remotely occurred to me that in making the star of my series a woman I had stumbled onto what at the time was a potentially marketable idea. Nor had I ever given the remotest thought to becoming a radio script writer—or a dramatist in any form.

I simply offered my brother Melvin a couple of my scripts to read. He thought well enough of them to pass them along to his literary agents, where one radio-oriented associate thought well enough of them to move a step further. Indeed, he saw the part as right for Hedda Hopper, a Broadway actress whom he knew. Miss Hopper was unemployed, as were hundreds of other actors and actresses, and it was well before her fortunes were to turn and she would rise to fame and fortune as a Hollywood columnist.

The agent, Miss Hopper and I met for luncheon to talk it over. I remember three things about it: (1) It took place at the Algonquin, famous as the writers' and actors' hotel, where I had never before been;

Portrait painted by a talented young artist named Day in early 1935 when both of us lived at New York's Henry Street Settlement. It became a prized possession, but when the artist asked for—and received—a fee of $15, I was hard pressed to scrape it up from my Depression-diminished resources . . . especially as I had assumed I was merely sitting as a "model."

(2) Miss Hopper seemed interested enough to think the prospect over; and (3) my newspaper-trained eye glimpsed a hole in the finger of one of her black gloves, leading me to recognize that these were not the best of times for Miss Hopper.

She took her time in thinking it over and I calmly prepared to dismiss the whole idea when sometime in late February or early March my potential as a script writer washed out with a call from Mary Routzahn. She had taken the liberty of arranging an appointment for me with Howard R. Knight, general secretary of the National Conference of Social Work (NCSW), the nation's oldest, largest social work membership organization—a trailblazer in the field of social welfare. He was interested in talking to me about a major position with the Conference.

The National Conference, dating back to the early years of modern social service, was organized in 1893 as the National Conference of Charities and Correction. In 1917, it adopted the name National Conference of Social Work. Still later (after my time), the name changed to the National Conference of Social Welfare, as it is presently known.

The upshot: after our initial meeting in New York and a visit to the national headquarters in Columbus, Ohio, to see and be seen, I was offered and accepted a prestigious position as the organization's first director of publicity.

What I was just starting to learn was the rising popular approval of the field I had entered. It was a time when social work and social workers, public and private social agencies and organizations were gaining new levels of recognition for their place in the social and economic structure. They were national news. And it would be my good fortune to have close association with many personalities who have taken their places in the history of the profession.

Ironically, just after the commitment was sealed, I learned that the Associated Press had been trying to reach me with an offer to join its Baltimore news bureau. This came out of a near-forgotten contact made soon after my arrival in New York with a friend of my brother's, a *Saturday Evening Post* editor and former newsman with abundant connections.

It was too late. I loaded the venerable little Ford, bade adieu to the Henry Street Settlement and my friends there and drove through the Alleghenies in a late-season snowstorm that blew the fabric top of the car into ribbons, landing in Columbus on April 1, 1935, in a continuation of that late-season storm.

So began career No. 2.

Chapter 16

And New Adventures

*M*y arrival in Columbus brought me to
National Conference headquarters with none too much time left to get
my bearings, to plan a meaningful formula for the sizable task ahead
and initiate publicity for its major event of the year, a huge national
meeting known as The Conference. This was—and continues to be—
the nationally recognized occasion in the welfare field, bringing together
thousands of social workers, public officials, educators, laymen and
laywomen to explore, discuss and evolve ways and means to effect social
improvement. Over the years, numerous social work organizations devoted to specialized phases of welfare have joined to meet under the
Conference umbrella. And so it was then.

Traditionally held in a different city each year, this Conference, the
first in my experience, was to take place in Montreal the last week in
May. Which left a bare seven weeks to go, including special attention
to newspapers around the country and the radio networks to encourage
coverage. For three of those weeks, key members of the organization
staff would be in the host city, as was customary, to complete prepa-
rations at the scene of action.

How did it all come out?

As I came to know, every Conference was a unique production.
Yet the formula held true for all. General Secretary Howard Knight
and his assistant, Jane Chandler, both established pros who had been
through it time and again, devoted much of each year to basic planning.
That meant working with social work leaders from many parts of the
country—who were volunteers in this role—developing the direction
and substance of the coming event, lining up speakers—as many as 400
or more who would address the various sessions—handling logistics so
effectively that hotels and meeting places would be ready for the thousands of delegates descending on the town from "everywhere" and

making provision for as many as 300 sessions in one week (20 or more taking place simultaneously)—all this with rarely a hitch.

Now a member of the inner circle, I too would be drawn in at various stages of advance planning, and that was my introduction to numerous personalities in the profession from many parts of the country. One of them, remembered for various pleasant reasons but especially for a display of remarkable memory, was Katharine F. Lenroot, chief of the U.S. Children's Bureau and president of the National Conference that year. It was at a major session of the upcoming annual meeting that she would deliver a spirited half-hour address before an audience of some 10,000—never once referring to her prepared manuscript (or to then-nonexistent cue cards).

As the Montreal Conference closed, there was warm applause on all counts: for the program, planning and publicity. Critics at all levels were generous in their comments on publicity, repeatedly calling it the most successfully publicized and interpreted Conference in memory. I can say that I felt good about it, too, and decided I was correct in what I had earlier surmised—that there is no substitute for a seasoned newspaper background.

It very soon became clear that an event as large as this, dispersed throughout the city . . . session after session addressed by nationally, internationally and regionally prominent speakers . . . newsworthy stories almost everywhere you turned . . . could scarcely be covered in depth by a single reporter (which a number of newspapers around the country, including the *New York Times,* assigned to it) or even a team of reporters which almost all of the eight English-language and French-language Montreal dailies assigned.

I devised a scheme to facilitate press coverage and make it possible for a newsman, if he chose, to cover the greater part of the Conference from our own press room. With the help of two or three knowledgeable news writers who were added to my staff for two weeks, we rewrote scores of yet-to-be presented speeches into news stories, holding them for release on the proper day. Beginning in advance of the opening of the Conference, the process continued until its close. What made it possible was a long-operative and successful effort on the part of the Conference staff to obtain speech manuscripts as far in advance as possible in preparation for the publication of an annual *Conference Proceedings*.

Coverage in Montreal newspapers far exceeded my most ardent dreams and delighted the delegates. Not only did the papers carry stories leading up to the opening, but two English-language dailies, the *Montreal Star* and the *Montreal Gazette,* published five and six full pages of Conference news every day of the week. Lead stories always were featured on page one. The French-language newspapers were not far behind. The press across the United States as well as Canada gave the Conference favorable attention, thanks to wire service reports and, for some papers, stories written by their own correspondents.

Newsreels covered it and network radio, notably NBC and CBS, carried a number of programs (those over NBC prearranged with Margaret Cuthbert, whom I had come to know in Henry Street Settlement days). Programs presented over local Montreal stations were so numerous that I long ago lost count. There were perhaps 25 or 30 or more.

Returning to Columbus in a euphoric mood, one of my first acts was to buy the handsome gunmetal gray Plymouth convertible that I had admired in the dealer's showroom window every time I passed on my way to and from the office. I traded in the valiant Ford. The deal will be no surprise if it is remembered that those were Depression days. The Plymouth cost a little less than $600, license and *everything* included. After dickering back and forth, the salesman and manager agreed to allow $149.49 for the Ford, explaining that (for reasons undisclosed) the company simply could not meet my firm demand for $150.

My year-round work with the National Conference was varied, including writing and editing the quarterly *Conference Bulletin,* a multipage magazine for members; directing membership recruitment; turning out brochures and other production pieces; interim publicity; and work on the next Conference.

But for me, it was the annual Conference that was the frosting on the cake, no matter how much work it demanded.

Twice in my early years with the Conference I received bids to join the new and expanding Information Service of the new and expanding Social Security system but elected to remain where I was. The first, in 1936, offered me a choice of informational directorships at various Social Security regional offices. When I declined I was chided by Louis Resnick, the national Informational Service director, whom I had come to know in New York. "Where," he demanded half in jest and all in earnest, "is your sense of patriotism?"

I remained with the National Conference for four years and five annual meetings. After Montreal came Atlantic City, Indianapolis, Seattle and Buffalo.

A remembered incident during the Seattle meeting was when Sanford Bates, director of the Bureau of Prisons of the U.S. Department of Justice, an acquaintance from my early Conference years, looked me up to introduce me to his Conference guest, former President Herbert C. Hoover. It was during Mr. Hoover's administration that the Bureau of Prisons was established.

It was in Montreal, however, that a series of encounters began with personalities who almost literally occupied a world stage. And every encounter was as memorable—and almost all as cherished—as any experienced in my life.

The first was with Eleanor Roosevelt. It became my welcome responsibility to greet her on her arrival as a Conference speaker and it was an exciting moment for me. Already famed as one of the world's foremost women, her participation had been announced in advance news stories and her visit was eagerly awaited in the city. Montrealers referred to her respectfully as our American "queen."

Times were simpler then. Unlike days to come, when Presidents, First Ladies and members of their families all would be shielded in their travels by details of Secret Service men, Mrs. Roosevelt arrived accompanied only by her frequent traveling companion, Nancy Cook. No Secret Service men, no motorcycle police escort, no Royal Mounties, no pomp, no ceremony.

As she stepped from a taxi at the entrance of the Mount Royal Hotel, it took only a moment for a crowd to gather around her (and me).

A newsreel cameraman had asked me to interview her on camera, and I approached her holding what in those days was a normal microphone—about equal in size to an artillery shell, connected to the camera via a thick cable.

Smiling, she told me what I had already been aware of: that she preferred not to be interviewed on camera (sensitive, as she was, about her high-pitched voice). But she was nevertheless gracious and communicative during the few minutes it took for the camera to record it all.

A fragmentary experience. But one never forgotten.

Eleanor Roosevelt interviewed by the author outside the Mount Royal Hotel, Montreal, in 1935. Mrs. Roosevelt's traveling companion, Nancy Cook, is at her right.

Quite the opposite—but no less memorable—was the experience with Secretary of Labor Frances Perkins, who addressed a general session, an evening occasion open not only to Conference delegates but to the general public. She shared the platform with the British High Commissioner to Canada, Sir Francis Flood and, as scheduled, preceded him.

This was a session the National Broadcasting Company wanted for a live pickup to be carried by its full network. Days earlier, in concluding arrangements with Margaret Cuthbert, she was explicit: NBC wanted only Sir Francis; it did *not* want Miss Perkins. And he was announced in the network's advance publicity.

Meeting with Miss Perkins a few hours before the session to review arrangements, I of course refrained from mentioning NBC's explicit instruction, rather, playing up its interest in Sir Francis, who would be making his maiden address to a U.S. audience. She said she clearly understood and willingly agreed to hold her speech to its allotted half hour and to close in time to permit her co-speaker to take the podium at 8:30, when the half-hour broadcast was to begin. Sir Francis was briefed on arrangements and was pleased with them.

Came evening. The session opened before an audience of some 10,000 in the old Montreal Forum. I took my place in the broadcast booth with the NBC announcer. Came 8:30 and Miss Perkins still held the podium. In the booth, the announcer began to read a background script, provided in case of need. Came 8:40, 8:43, 8:45, etc., etc., with Miss Perkins still holding forth.

Finally running out of delaying tactics, the announcer switched to Miss Perkins with a brief comment as the clock neared 8:50. Sir Francis never made it on the air. My conclusion, shared by others of the Conference family, was that Miss Perkins knew precisely what was going on and determined that if anyone was to be on the air that night it would be she.

In all the long years since that night, Miss Perkins' fame as the first U.S. woman cabinet member has been overshadowed for me by her demonstrated failure in mannerly behavior.

Presumably, Sir Francis was unaware that his scheduled time on the air had been preempted by the first speaker: the NBC mike was in place throughout his appearance, though not live. For my part, the situation was too painful to consider offering an apology—even to consider mentioning it unless asked. How do you explain away such a performance by a ranking member of the President's cabinet?

I simply went up to him at the close of the meeting after he had received the compliments of his platform sharers, including Conference president Miss Lenroot, to add my appreciation for his address, which indeed went extremely well, the audience responding enthusiastically.

He was totally gracious, wondering only if I would care to join him and Lady Flood in a walk in the lovely evening air to their hotel. Of course, I would and did.

I remember it as a pleasant, chatty stroll but can recall only one small fragment of the conversation. That was when Sir Francis asked whether by any chance I was originally from his homeland, Britain; the clarity of my speech seemed to impress him. The remark came as a total surprise. No, I assured him, the speech I spoke came out of Northwest United States.

Another long-remembered incident occurred the day the Conference was closing. I left our press room on a mission of good cheer, a visit to the Provincial liquor store to buy some choice alcoholic beverages as a token of appreciation for members of the press who had been such good companions and splendid reporters. Leaving the store, both arms bulging with paper bags of liquor, I had taken no more than a dozen steps when I walked head-on into a familiar figure whose large frame, bushy mustache and ready smile told me it was an old friend from Seattle whom I had not seen in years—Vernon McKenzie, dean of the School of Journalism at the University of Washington. My arms were too full for a proper handshake nor could I stand too long holding a load that was taxing my muscles. I had no question that the dean knew what I was carrying—though not why—but pretended he didn't, and I offered no explanation. He was on his way to England on a writing assignment. Our remarks were brief but friendly and he went his way and I mine. We would see each other again and again in Seattle. But never a mention of Montreal.

McKenzie and I had a special relationship dating from my senior year when, self-motivated, he overruled a School of Journalism directive that he—and I—considered stuffy for an institution of higher learning. That was a requirement, which I never fulfilled, calling for a course in shorthand or demonstrated shorthand proficiency as a prerequisite to graduation. Aware of my overabundance of credits in more meaningful subjects, he simply obtained my diploma and delivered it to me after I left the campus.

On reflection, I never encountered a newsman or woman who employed any shorthand beyond his or her individual brand of cryptographics.

Then there was Indianapolis, with two especially memorable experiences.

One involved Senator Robert F. Wagner of New York, famed among other reasons for his key role in pushing enactment of New Deal legislation, including the act that bore his name, the Wagner Labor Relations Act; the other, Frank Murphy, then governor of Michigan, later a liberally oriented justice of the U.S. Supreme Court. The year: 1937. Both men were scheduled to address Conference general sessions.

Senator Wagner had submitted an advance copy of his speech, which I read with dismay, considering it much too weak for a man of his stature in that historic time. I took the manuscript to Jane M. Hoey, director of the Bureau of Public Assistance of the Social Security Board, a long-time friend of his—and a less-long but good friend of mine—who was attending the Conference. She agreed to call him in Washington and urge that he spruce it up. But no word of changes was received.

On his arrival in Indianapolis, I met the senator at the railroad station and, having instructed the taxi driver to take a roundabout route to the senator's hotel, spent a long half hour pointing out areas of his speech that I felt needed strengthening, to assure him of the headlines he deserved. He took it all in good part, agreeing to consider the matter.

Reaching the hotel, we discovered that the world had changed. The Indianapolis newspapers were on the street with blazing headlines announcing that the U.S. Supreme Court had upheld the Wagner Labor Relations Act. For my part, I instantly saw that I was dealing with the man of the hour, who could recite a page from *Alice in Wonderland* at the evening session and still claim front-page position in newspapers throughout the nation. What we did was to set up a news conference for him forthwith at the headquarters hotel. It bulged with newsmen. Both of us dismissed the idea of making changes in the speech he was to deliver that night.

The experience with Governor Murphy was another that consumed only a fragment of time.

The day before his scheduled Conference address, I was getting uneasy. His speech manuscript had not arrived, and he was far too important a national figure not to receive as much advance preparation as possible.

So I called the Governor's office in Lansing, hoping to speak to a secretary who might expedite matters. It was a man's voice on the other end. Pausing only for the briefest moment of indecision—I had not expected a male secretary—I asked to speak to Governor Murphy.

Relaxed moment on the Atlantic City Boardwalk as the author meets three social workers attending the 1936 meeting of the National Conference of Social Work.

"This," he replied, "is Governor Murphy."

Stating my business briefly and receiving assurance that he would have his manuscript with him on his arrival in Indianapolis the next day, I offered my telephone number and asked: "Would you call me when you reach your hotel?"

I could sense the Governor rising to full height as he responded with appropriate dignity: "I suggest that you call me."

Which closed the conversation.

Finally, one tiny incident in a day in the life of one of America's distinguished leaders of the time, Fiorello H. LaGuardia, the much-esteemed, free-spirited mayor of New York. It happened before my eyes, and I have cherished it ever since.

The time: June 1939. The mayor flew into Buffalo in the afternoon to deliver a major address before a general session of the National Conference. Afterward, he was to fly to Washington to testify the next morning before the Senate Committee on Appropriations in behalf of a Works Project Administration (WPA) bill.

Crowded into his agenda was a significant third item in which I had a direct hand. It was a one-of-a-kind National Broadcasting Company radio network program: a ship-to-shore conversation between the mayor in a Buffalo studio and Sir Percy Bates, chairman of the Cunard Line, who was sailing across the Atlantic aboard the new Cunard White Star liner *Mauretania* on her maiden voyage from Liverpool to New York.

The broadcast scheduled to take place an hour before the evening general session was to begin, a fairly tight schedule, I accompanied Mr. LaGuardia to the studio with two principal objectives in mind. One was to encourage him and the studio announcer to weave meaningful comments on the National Conference of Social Work into the ad-lib, free-wheeling conversation (in which I succeeded); the other, to make sure of the mayor's arrival at Broadway Auditorium and a capacity audience at the appointed hour. This also succeeded.

Having time to kill before the broadcast, the announcer asked Mr. LaGuardia if he would care to don a pair of earphones and listen to the program under way. Indeed he would, and he was seated in a large armchair drawn up to a spacious studio table, a microphone—not yet activated—in place before him.

A man of short stature—his feet did not quite touch the floor—he sat swinging his legs as he listened through the earphones. In a

Mayor Fiorello H. LaGuardia, arriving at Buffalo Airport, hands copy of his National Conference address to the author. Between us: Frank Murphy, my assistant. Right: Helen Hall of the Henry Street Settlement, also arriving for the Conference. The scene, with action reflected in a highly-polished automobile, was caught by a Buffalo Courier Express *photographer and appeared on page one of the newspaper.*

sudden flash of sheer ecstasy, he laughed and half-shouted: "It's the Lone Ranger! My little boy Eric is listening to him at home this very minute!"

Savoring the moment to the end, Mr. LaGuardia was prompted into action by the announcer, and the ship-to-shore conversation went on the air. The next morning I received a congratulatory telegram from Margaret Cuthbert expressing pleasure with the program that she and I had concocted.

And Back to New York

Events preceding the Buffalo Conference were joyful for many reasons: most of all for my marriage to the lovely and bright Alice Klund. She had graduated from Ohio Wesleyan University in 1932 and embarked almost immediately on a promising career, becoming the first paid executive secretary of the League of Women Voters (LWV) in her home city, Erie, Pennsylvania, and simultaneously regional secretary for the Northwest Pennsylvania LWV. She came to Columbus in 1936 as executive secretary of the Columbus and Franklin County League of Women Voters. We met soon afterward and married in September 1938.

Among various likes and dislikes we shared was a hearty distaste for Columbus as a place to live. Despite the presence of two universities within the city . . . despite an aspiring art museum and a symphony orchestra . . . despite its being the state capital . . . the spark that both of us had expected to find there never ignited. It was a story repeated by other newcomers who found the city intellectually dormant. If a city can be characterized as complacent and self-satisfied, that was Columbus in the 1930s.

Toward the end of our days there, we learned to our surprise and initial disbelief that it even had an unwritten but rigidly enforced code separating residents on religious grounds. Jewish families lived on the older east side, while the west side, including Bexley and other newer areas near the Olentangy River, was reserved for WASPs.

It was a very personal discovery, made on our return to Columbus as newlyweds. Determining, as I did, that my bachelor apartment near Ohio State University—reasonably comfortable as it was—was not good enough for my lovely bride, we set out to find a proper apartment, concentrating the search on the newer west side.

139

And we thought we found it almost at once. The elderly couple who showed it to us displayed pleasure in learning that their tenants-to-be were newly married. We did not know whether they were owners or managers. Details for moving in were arranged—until they asked our name. Confused and apologetic, they informed us that, regretfully, we could not have it. They accepted Christians only. And so it went as our search progressed and we picked up advice that we might try the east side of town.

It was only when a prominent League of Women Voters friend and her well-established physician husband took it upon themselves to certify our worthy character and persuaded one landlord to ease the rule that we were able to rent a pleasant apartment in the pleasant and convenient west side.

Far from crushing us, the experience merely added to our disdain for the city, proving to us once again how Columbus consistently fell short of its potentials. Beyond that, we knew that it would never be "our" city, and we lived with the experience.

Then, sooner than anticipated, everything changed.

In early 1939, Mary Routzahn of the Russell Sage Foundation paid a visit to Columbus and to us, bringing a shaft of light.

She came to prevail upon me to join the Russell Sage Foundation as a research associate in the department she directed, the Department of Social Work Interpretation.

The Russell Sage Foundation had been established in New York in 1907, a time when foundations were still a novelty in America; only eight were then in existence. It was the gift, among other benefactions, of the widow of the man for whom it was named, who left his entire fortune of $65 million to her. Its purpose, as set forth in the articles of incorporation, was to work for the improvement of social and living conditions in the United States, using any and all expedient means to that end, including research, publication, education and establishment and maintenance of charitable or benevolent activities, agencies and institutions. Its impact on the well-being of the nation has been un-ending. To mention only a random few examples: fostering legislation that brought usurious lending practices to an end; fostering credit unions, mine safety, improved working conditions for women; pi-oneering work in the conquest of tuberculosis; launching the Camp Fire Girls and various other recreational and health movements—and not the least, its untiring activity directed to social work interpretation:

Alice, 1983.

creating techniques and methods that are the basis of much of today's professional practice of public relations. (See *The Russell Sage Foundation, 1907–1946,* by John M. Glenn, Lilian Brandt and F. Emerson Andrews [New York: Russell Sage Foundation, 1947], 2 vols.)

I was Mary Routzahn's choice to carry out a project that she had long envisioned: to conduct original research leading to books that would become the first published case studies in the field of public relations, a field which in those days was a developing, but still unformed and often random, specialty. The focus of our studies would, of course, be on the field of social welfare.

The prospect would have been too tempting to resist under any circumstances: an offer to participate in exploring—possibly even having a hand in shaping—a field that was barely coming into its own. Even the descriptive term *public relations* was so far behind the popular awareness it would attain in a generation or two that a considerable part of the practitioner's role in those days was to explain the term— and more significantly, to "sell" what was involved in technical application of public relations in business and industry, no less than in social welfare. Unlike days to come, there was little, if any, formal education in the field, let alone university degrees.

It was Mrs. Routzahn's hope to get under way with minimum delay.

Alice and I were enchanted with the idea. We left Columbus in March 1939 for the attractive Manhattan apartment near Gramercy Park that would be home for the nearly 10 years of our New York sojourn.

To compensate for my departure from the National Conference so near its approaching annual meeting, it was mutually and amicably agreed that I would take leave of the Foundation long enough to direct publicity for the Buffalo Conference. Thus, my relations with the Conference ended on a high note.

━━━━━━━━━━━━━━━

Chapter 17

Reflections

*P*erhaps the time comes for everyone. In any case, for me the time for self-examination began in early adulthood and continued over a protracted period.

Let it be noted that neither the calendar nor the clocks stood still. Life, work, ambition, achievements, disappointments, pleasures, gains and losses continued without interruption.

Even as a small child I was shy, and I came to know that the effects of this shyness were long lasting.

I know that the trait was not inherited. My father was not a timid man. Although a child does not really pay attention to the physical attributes or the attitudes of a parent, merely accepting and embracing them, I am aware that he always seemed in control of situations. I remember him in his earlier days as a tall, good-looking man who had a way of ingratiating himself with others, just as, to me, my mother was always pretty and gentle and able to handle situations with ease.

Even as his weight increased during his thirties and forties and more markedly in his fifties, his sense of humor, his engaging way with jokes, banter and stories impressed, indeed charmed, the ladies—the ladies being family friends or those encountered in social and business situations—who reacted spontaneously and favorably to him. To my lifelong knowledge he never philandered. He simply had a gift for winning friends. It never occurred to me to envy him.

I came to know that my shyness was selective. Whenever I had a meaningful responsibility to perform, I could be as brave or bold as anyone. But I could be struck mute with timidity at other times.

It was two weeks after starting piano lessons at, I think, age 6 that I was told by Mrs. Sigmond, my teacher, that I was to participate in a recital in coming days. And when the time came, all of it went off without a trace of embarrassment. Attending the affair in her home were perhaps 50 parents and pupils, among the latter several accomplished performers. As first on the program, I carried my music book to the piano, sat, opened it to the proper page and played two "pieces," the first 15 notes long, the second 18. Retaking my place, I acknowledged the applause with a slight bow, as I had been instructed to do, and felt perfectly calm and pleased.

Yet two or three years later as a more "accomplished" pianist, I wilted with embarrassment when asked by my parents to play before guests in our own home, unfailingly fading from the scene without touching the keyboard.

Nor was I timid when my "rights" or "honor" were at stake. I have a clear memory of such a day when an eighth grader at Stevens Elementary School. For reasons completely lost to memory, a classmate and I had some kind of word battle at recess and promised to fight it out after school.

Neither of us was endowed with fighting skill, but we came to blows on a parking strip lawn, whether fortunately or otherwise, in full view of our eighth grade classroom. We were in a rolling, wrestling match, each determined to do the other in, when our teacher appeared on the scene and stopped the fracas. She did all the appropriate things, reprimanding us and, failing to learn what the fight was all about, seeing to it that we shook hands—and sent us on our separate ways home. I think my classmate and I were satisfied that we had proved ourselves and let the chips fall from our shoulders.

There were many incidents when, without conscious thought, either timidity or mettle prevailed, seemingly determined by some inner awareness that passed instant judgment.

As a high school freshman, shyness was put aside as I entered the race for class secretary, carrying my campaign to "the people." A few evenings at home were given over to hand-printing election signs plumping LEVY FOR SECRETARY, and my campaign manager assisted in posting them in the school hallways. It may be said that my manager, a fellow freshman named Dave Lewis, knew no more about campaign managing than I; it never occurred to us to find an "issue." I delivered a campaign speech before a class assembly—and lost the election to a classmate, Jack McWalter, whose speech was far more rousing and evocative than mine: well deserving the vote he received. In latter years, Jack became a lawyer. We would encounter each other occasionally, retaining friendly relations.

As years passed, my shyness diminished, though I was in my late twenties before it slowly—though perhaps not completely—dissipated.

Above all, however, in my life as a newsman and, later, as public relations practitioner, it was as though I was commanded by a different force—one without tolerance for timidity. From my days as fledgling publisher of the *Capital Cub* onward, I was perfectly at ease, totally unself-conscious in performing my cherished responsibilities. And so it was, and is, throughout my public relations career.

To my unremitting dismay, it was with girls and young women on a social level that bravery wavered.

Looking back from the vantage point of later years, I can find no sound explanation beyond a number of witless foibles, one or another surfacing at what I can only think were crucial moments. Among them, my innate tendency toward shyness in interpersonal relations, combined with fear that I was not quite up to the requisite small talk . . . uncertainty that a girl really meant what seemed initial interest . . . failure to respond to certain lovely women when hindsight tells me I should have . . . long periods of financial insecurity . . . lack of courage to even try dancing because I "knew" I couldn't do it—until Alice ultimately took me in hand and converted me into a passable performer on the dance floor . . . an unnerving concern that if a relationship were to proceed to the ultimate and I contracted a disease I could be lost in trying to cope with it.

I should have received a failing grade—a plain F—in boy-girl and young man–young woman relations had anyone been on hand to score my performance in repudiated opportunities.

It was not until my late twenties that I began to see the error of my ways.

I have never forgotten my initial (and rejected) opportunity. She was a lovely young woman. Her husband, a newspaper contemporary and friend, was out of the city and she invited me to Sunday dinner, to remain through the long evening, and finally (I being such a novice at it) she initiated the idea of making love. Being less than the red-blooded American boy I might have wished, I urged that she settle for a passionate kiss or two and departed, clearly to her disappointment. I remember how late it was. It was before I had a car, the streetcars had stopped running for the night and I had a walk of four or five miles home. Knowing that I would have to rise by 5 o'clock to get to my early morning post at police headquarters, I spent the walk mulling over the experience.

Some nine months later, I recognized that I was spared a future of uncertainty. She bore a daughter, and I knew I had been relieved of years of wonder as to whether the child could be mine.

Then there was the charming girl to whom I was introduced shortly before my second vacation trip by sea to Los Angeles, this time aboard the sleek SS *H. F. Alexander*. Mutual friends felt we should meet because she, too, was to make the same trip. She was employed in the advertising department of the *Seattle Times* and was a niece of one of the ranking editors. I felt that she was aware of me before we met.

My experiences aboard ship, although limited, had taught me that shipboard could be a romantic paradise for those who wished it to be. A tempting prospect. But I knew that whatever her innermost thoughts may have been, mine were to avoid entanglement. Happily, there were many other diversions. The evening before the end and our return home, we talked late into the night. Looking into my eyes, she told how much she regretted having the trip end. I remember how pretty she was and the dress she wore: dark blue embellished with little white stars.

Thereafter, she invited me to her home to meet her widowed father with whom she lived, and repeated the invitation. It was pleasant but not a relationship I could pursue. And it all tapered off.

There was the time in Columbus when a rap sounded on my apartment door late one evening as I sat reading. I lived alone. My caller was an extremely attractive dark-haired young woman from across the hall. I had taken note of her in neighborly fashion, but did not know her name. She entered clad in a temptingly filmy negligee. She said her husband was out of town, she was lonely and wanted to talk a bit. But talk was hardly the word for it. I decided she was—or had been—a dancer, for she executed a beautiful leg-stretched routine while standing almost en pointe. And I thought what a pity it was—she married to a rather stuffy-appearing man. A traveling salesman? A junior executive immersed in the world of business? I had seen him, too, but did not know him or his name.

Brushing temptation aside, I shortly decided that the encounter should end and escorted her to the darkened back porch, which opened on both her apartment and mine. We kissed and bade goodnight. Fortunately, the couple soon moved and I never saw her again.

And there was a rememberable encounter in Montreal with an extremely winning young woman, not really pretty but gifted with an exciting presence. She worked with one of the local social agencies that cooperated in staging the big National Conference. Our paths crossed frequently and there was no question that we were mutually attracted. On a day near the end of the week-long meetings, pressures diminishing, she accepted an invitation for a late-afternoon refreshment in the hotel cocktail lounge. We stopped in my room at the Mount Royal to freshen up. And we lingered. And lingered. And she said, "I know what we both want." And she was right. But again, I held back. And it ended with an affectionate kiss.

Finally, remember Denton, Texas, where I spent one night on my trip east?

It was a truly romantic full-moon night, and I lingered in a sitting area in front of the tourist court, well aware of an attractive young woman, older than I—but not *that* old—and a man I judged to be a local swain. I outstayed their tête-à-tête, certain that she glanced my way from time to time.

When she was alone again, we talked for a few minutes and as midnight approached I reluctantly bade her goodnight. I learned then what I had surmised: that she was the daughter of the proprietors of the tourist court.

Would I like to have her show me to my cabin? she asked.

Of course, I would.

And she did.

Then came my crucial moment of decision—whether the right one or not I am not certain that I ever knew.

We pushed open the screen door and entered the cabin, pausing in the dark for a moment of passionate kissing. Then I edged her slightly toward the entrance.

Clearly nonplussed, she asked, "Is that all you want?"

We kissed again. I opened the door and she departed.

Happily, such unfinished adventures came to an end when Alice and I met in Columbus.

From almost the first moment I sensed this was it: the first girl I really ever wanted to marry.

With understandable interruptions, there was scarcely a day thereafter when we failed to see each other or at least to talk by telephone.

I took pleasure in sending her flowers, stirring what she told me was amiable jealousy among other young women living, as she did, at the Columbus YWCA. We dined together frequently and danced to a live orchestra at what then was the prestigious Deshler-Wallick Hotel. She invited me to visit her family home in Erie, Pennsylvania, to meet her parents and other family members—there also to meet at least two suitors who had aspirations of marrying her. On weekends, we often drove the beautiful, rolling mid-Ohio countryside, which was alive not only with handsomely maintained farms but, in one village and small city after another, more small colleges and universities than I believed possible.

It was a continual round of adventures and many happy incidents: the memory of one never failing to delight us. It was a sunny Saturday afternoon and we were driving a lonely back country road. Perhaps a quarter mile ahead we took note of a man, clearly a farmer, outside a picket fence. As we approached, he flagged us down.

His was a sad story. Returning from his weekly shopping trip to some miles-away town, he discovered that he had forgotten to make one crucially important purchase.

Revealing his problem, he asked whether I had any chewing tobacco.

No chewing tobacco, I replied, but in those days being an avid pipe smoker, I offered my pouch full of pipe tobacco, and we shared the contents.

Beaming with the joy of a man redeemed, he leaned in and asked: "Would you like a drink of goddam fine whisky?" Whether it was his own make or not we never knew. We thanked him warmly and said we had better be on our way.

If a new friendship can be sealed in a single moment, that one was. Waving us on with a cordial goodbye, he turned and walked briskly to his farm home.

It was in the summer of 1938, and Alice departed on a long-planned trip, in large part a cycling venture through much of Europe: England, the Scandinavian countries, Italy, Austria and way points, all with a group of young men and women who were university students or recent graduates.

She was gone for a long two months—the longest separation since we had been introduced on Armistice Day, November 11, 1936, by a mutual friend who invited us to cocktails at a downtown hotel, then judiciously departed.

In early September, I met her ship, the Holland-American SS *Volandam,* on its arrival in New York and asked her to marry me.

The wedding took place just one week later, out-of-doors in Bucks County, Pennsylvania, at my brother and sister-in-law's summer place overlooking the Delaware River: his writing retreat. We have our long-standing joke, saying the ceremony was performed under a peach tree. But as any tree fancier would know, no peach tree could accommodate a wedding party under its branches. It was indeed *beside* a peach tree. Presiding was the local justice of the peace, known there as squire: Squire Moyer, a robust 80-year-old country-raised gentleman who gave us joy as we watched him stride across fields carrying his large law book under arm. Alice remembers that he outdid her at the wedding breakfast where sister-in-law Peggy served her long-pined-for menu—hamburgers. In a sense, it was a race for the burgers between the good squire and the bride.

The wedding night was perfect: under a mellow full moon at the romantic Washington Crossing Inn on the Delaware, marking the point where General Washington and his troops crossed on their victorious march on Trenton. The date: September 8, 1938.

Then a leisurely driving trip via Erie to Columbus and the surprised welcome by friends and associates.

Chapter 18

Once in New York, one of the great adventures of our life together began.

For me: Research that took me to many parts of the country visiting social agencies of all sizes and descriptions, interviewing and exploring attitudes, objectives, training, backgrounds and the varied techniques applied to achieving—or failing to achieve—popular understanding and goodwill for the agencies and their roles in society. And writing two books published by the Russell Sage Foundation.

For Alice: Having given up a professional career with the League of Women Voters, she became an active volunteer, being elected successively to the boards of directors of the New York City and New York State Leagues.

For both of us: Living in New York in one of its truly exhilarating times, it was an unending succession of adventures. Broadway plays—which were abundant and at the time easily available—ballet, music, museums, art galleries, libraries, zoos, waterfronts, marvelous stores and shops, fine restaurants, an opportunity to explore the city's and the nation's abundant historic sites dating from Colonial days, the pleasure of strolling Broadway, Fifth Avenue, Madison Avenue, the Lower East Side, Greenwich Village, the Battery and all the others, always colorful, always safe day and night. And all the abundant, enduring friendships!

Perhaps because we sensed—or knew—that New York was not to be our permanent home, we were forever open-eyed, eager to take in as much as possible, ever ready for exploration and adventure. Explorations were for the most part self-generated. As for the adventures, we simply were always ready and fell in with them as they opened up. And we savored every encounter.

One of our most delectable adventures occurred on a very cold, bright Saturday in February when we decided it was a good day to take a ferry ride across the Hudson River: at that time not only a refreshing but a splendidly inexpensive trip—a nickel per passenger each way or simply a nickel if you chose to stay aboard rather than disembark on the Jersey side.

Boarding the *Stony Point*—a name to be remembered ever after—at Manhattan's 42nd Street ferry slip, we chose to sit in the snug, spacious, virtually deserted upper cabin. Minding our own affairs, we presently became aware of a man walking through the cabin, who paused to mumble something to us.

Looking up with a "pardon us, what did you say?" both of us took note that he was a medium-small older man wearing a near-seedy dark blue suit and a nautical cap embroidered "captain" in gold thread.

"Would you like to ride across with me in the pilot house?"

Would we! And we did.

His name, he said, was Captain Tom Deming.

Although near retirement, he said, he wanted to obey new orders issued by the Weekauken–Manhattan ferry line's parent, the New Jersey Central Railroad. And he pulled a much-folded mimeographed letter from a breast pocket, reading us an excerpt that instructed company personnel to be courteous to passengers. No doubt a communication inspired by the company's budding public relations department.

Included in his hospitality were cups of coffee poured from a pot resting on a hot steam register. Also instructions to Alice on boxing the compass and—literally—steering the vessel. And a word of caution: When the first mate appeared we would be introduced as the captain's niece and nephew. Indeed, the first mate did appear, scowling at the sight of guests in the inner sanctum of the pilot house.

As the mate departed after a growly exchange between the two, the captain laughingly told us not to be concerned, adding that the younger man, Tom Braddock's brother, always looked that way. Tom Braddock was at the time the reigning heavyweight champion of the world.

About that time, both of us began to wonder whether the good captain had taken a warming snort sometime before our meeting, was determined to have companionship in his sometimes lonely pursuit, or, in his own way, was following company instructions. But we never doubted that he was well in command.

Once across the river, we were invited to join him in the pilot house at the opposite end of the ferry. We did. And so it went for four or five round trips when, the day waning, we expressed deep thanks and wishes for a happy retirement and disembarked where it all began.

But the day was not yet finished.

Walking away, we heard a call from the rear, turned and saw Captain Deming, hands cupped, shouting through an open pilot house window. "Just had orders to sail 'er down to the Battery. Want to go along for the ride?"

Whereupon we retraced our steps and headed for our longest trip of the day.

No doubt considering that his hospitality still had a way to go, the captain sighted a liner sailing downriver, perhaps Europe-bound, and decided to race it. It was clear that the *Stony Point* was no match for the liner even though the huge ship traveled at reduced speed. But the captain made a go of it, blasting his horn at smaller boats to clear the way. And for Alice: further instruction in boxing the compass.

Until in the early dusk we reached the Battery, once more bade the captain adieu and made our way home via subway.

Our remaining years in New York were exciting and upbeat.

We were there to experience the victorious end of World War II, both the European and Japanese phases, and to see the enormous parades of returning soldiers: and always riding in the lead, the heroic generals whose names were already recorded in the histories of the times. We also saw—and grieved with—a city in mourning on the death of Franklin Roosevelt: shop windows the length of Manhattan's Fifth Avenue and adjacent streets given over to draped memorials to the dead President and an endless flow of muted strollers pausing to view them. We saw St. Patrick's Day parades along Fifth Avenue— rollicking sights that you had to see to believe if you were brought up elsewhere in the country. And the Easter parades that brought out lavish displays of finery in the crowds strolling Fifth Avenue. Alice and I were observers on one such occasion when a puzzled woman addressed a policeman standing near us. "I thought there was going to be a parade," she said. "Where is it?"

And he replied, "Lady, you're looking at it."

For me there were various ranking job offers, one of which was finally tempting enough to take. I departed the Foundation at the end of 1944 to become public relations director of a new social science research organization called the Commission on Community Interrelations (CCI). It brought together an elite corps of "name" social scientists from many parts of the nation as advisers. Its function: to perform what it named "action research," studying causes and effects of intergroup tensions and, as part of the study process, creating small teams of researchers to work on solutions in real-life situations. Thus, research in action: action research.

My part in it was deemed successful, among other reasons, for obtaining national recognition for the organization within months of its founding: for example, in engineering a feature article in the old *Collier's* magazine before CCI's first birthday and within the same period staging a news conference that fulfilled a generally held dream: a major news story in the *New York Times*.

Soon I received another tempting offer; this from one of the nation's leading advertising agencies, Young & Rubicam, to join its newly developing public relations department in a major role. For better or for worse (and despite a sometime pang of wistfulness, I have considered it for the better), I declined the offer.

Ultimately, nostalgia for the West overcame me. I resigned my position with CCI and, in 1947, we took a step that both Alice and I heartily embraced and moved to Los Angeles. This was a city I had come to know through many visits and where I was known, particularly in educational and welfare fields, through my connections with the National Conference of Social Work and the Russell Sage Foundation and my first two public relations books.

Our purpose was to enable me to establish a public relations firm of my own. Which I did, only to encounter a mix of early struggle and ultimate success: never, however, doubting the wisdom either of returning to the West or of embracing my second career.

Thanks again to a protective fate—or luck—it was my good fortune soon after settling into our new surroundings to receive a fairly prestigious appointment, and it had positive effects. I was invited to plan and present the first course in public relations to be offered by the University of California Extension, the big off-campus arm of the University of California. It was an evening class, meeting once a week, therefore handleable.

A friend in New York, an educator, had been lured to the UCLA faculty at about the same time we moved West, and we enjoyed a reunion in Los Angeles. Without consulting me—but with my belated blessings—he arranged an invitation for me to meet the dean of UCLA's business school to discuss why and how a school such as his should broaden its curriculum to give specific attention to that developing specialty, public relations. When it took place, the meeting was not simply between the dean and me. He had assembled eight or nine key faculty members to join in a roundtable discussion. It was formidable and a new experience for me—an educational tyro endeavoring to "sell" a new subject to a group of seasoned professors considering a subject new to them and peppering me with more questions than I could readily answer.

At that time, the opportunity for formal education in public relations was meager at best. Boston University broke ground in 1947 when it offered the nation's first academic degree program in public relations. Otherwise few if any colleges and universities in the entire country presented even a single course in the subject: a state of being that would change radically in one educational generation.

My encounter with the gentlemen of the business school ended at best, I thought, indecisively. But there clearly was more ruboff than I thought. For soon came the invitation from the University of California Extension and my involvement as an instructor from 1947 through 1949, when I resigned.

Soon afterward, my third book was written in response to word from Harper & Brothers that they were seeking a book focused on public relations for social agencies. It was published in 1956.

Belatedly—and to my surprise—I was to find in my early years in Los Angeles that we had come to a part of the country where the blossoming profession I was into was little known to business, industry or organizations of any kind. A few banks, a few corporations had public relations managers—the forerunner of the divisions and departments that were yet to come.

What I gained was the stimulating pleasure of taking part with a handful of other public relations pioneers in creating a presence for this profession.

Chapter 19

*O*ne day in 1942, an unexpected but highly welcome visitor called on me in my Russell Sage Foundation office in New York. He was Henry MacLeod, one-time colleague on the *Seattle Times,* who had joined the editorial staff as a rewrite man sometime after my arrival on the paper. We were contemporaries in age and warm friends. He was now city editor of the *Times,* destined in a few years to rise to managing editor.

We talked at length about Seattle in the past and the Seattle that was then thriving almost beyond belief in World War II years.

He then got around to inviting me to come to Seattle to write a series of articles on the city as a war-boom town, contrasted with the way it was when I left in 1934. The Army had already turned thumbs down on me as a soldier, a decision made, to my surprise, on the basis of a skull fracture received some time before in an accident. So I was free to accept.

Henry's proposal seemed a delightful prospect, and Alice and I chose two weeks in August—half of my then-one-month-long vacation—for the venture.

It was old home week (or two weeks) for me and a happy experience for Alice: a wonderful time visiting old friends—who were her new friends—and a free hand to range the area and write a daily feature that appeared under my byline.

"Take it from someone who happened to make both trips: The Hudson River is a lot nearer Puget Sound than the Seattle of 1934 is to the Seattle of 1942."

Such was my overriding impression . . . and such were the opening words of the first feature story written for the *Seattle Times* on my return as an observer-writer-commentator after a lapse of eight years (or a millennium?).

"Have a look," the story continued.

> You board a train and head westward, and as the wheels start clicking off those 3,000-plus miles from Grand Central Station to King Street Station, you remember Seattle of the depression period, eight, nine, ten years ago: Seattle as you last saw it. Breadlines in the skidroad district; breadlines maintained by a few of the social agencies that helped to keep thousands of down-and-outers from starving. The 'hunger march' in February, 1933, when 3,500 men, women and children camped in the King County Courthouse for two and a half days and the county's administrative government closed shop until the marchers finally were evicted. The waterfront strikes, and officers racing to the piers by the scores. Seattle was in the dumps then, and that's the way you saw it . . .
>
> Of course, as you ride across the country you know that's far in the past. But you wonder how far. Magazines and newspapers have been telling about Seattle, the war-boom town. *Business Week* the other day told what a lusty, thriving place it is—so many swing-shift workers in the war factories that restaurants are busy serving breakfasts all day long. *Time* magazine told how Boeing has 40,000 workers and is going to hire a lot more as soon as its new, big plant is finished. . . .

That was merely the opening of two weeks of discovery and writing, a period of uninhibited exploration and enormous pleasure.

Then on another day:

> The job market in this war-boom city is like a great big basket of prize packages, and every package holds a solid gold loving cup.
>
> Everyone who wants work is working and jobs are going begging. Money is rolling into the family exchequer. Dad is bringing it home and so is Mom. The youngsters are working like beavers. And there is employment for Grandma, too, if only she will take it . . .
>
> People are feeling good about this new prosperity—even though it is tinged with the grimness of war—and talk about it. You hear it in stores, factories, streets, busses, offices and homes. The clerk in a Fourth Avenue drug store heard of Seattle's boom several months ago while working in Little Rock, Ark., and decided to see for herself. She was getting $12 a week for similar work "back home." She draws $27.50 and commissions here.

Three partners in a Pike Street barber shop are closing the establishment they set up years ago, two of them to work in the shipyards, the third to accept a job in a large barber shop, where he has been offered more money than he had been earning as his own boss. . . .

And again:

Wander around Seattle with your wife if you want to get the woman's angle in this war-boom city.

You can see for yourself that the girls and women walking briskly along the Seattle streets are as pulchritudinous a lot as in 1934, when (without a wife at your side) you took careful note of such matters . . .

But you will have to depend upon your wife to point out that Seattle women wear darker clothes and fewer white shoes than their sisters in the East. She noticed that right away . . .

Getting off the subject of women and frocks and getting aboard one of Seattle's trolley coaches, you both note how smoothly and swiftly and comfortably it rides. You recall how those old lumbering street cars used to grumble and creak through the Seattle streets when you last saw the city in 1934.

You both find yourselves comparing the Seattle busses with those of New York and, aside from agreeing that the 5-cent fare on Manhattan's coaches holds a marked edge over the 8⅓-cent rate in Seattle, you decide you get a better ride for your money here . . . .

And a story dealing with wartime housing projects:

In its amazing new housing developments, Seattle has carved a living monument to the times—and that is one of the most important stories of this city at war.

When you recall the wilderness of raw land, woods and marshes which have been converted within a few brief years—or months—into home sites for hundreds or thousands of war workers, the story becomes twice as exciting.

Take one of the federally-financed housing projects, for example: Rainier Vista Homes. You used to drive past that site at Empire Way and Columbian Way when it was a bog . . .

Now it is a terraced residential area, dotted with groups and clusters of brightly painted single-story homes where 500 Boeing workers and shipyard workers and their families live. Two hundred thirty-one multiple-family houses, and every one of them tenanted. But those modern, oil-heated homes ranging in rent from a modest wartime scale of $33.75 for a single-bedroom unit to $40.25 for three bedrooms, present only part of the story.

157

There is a community house out at Rainier Vista. And there is a lot of what used to be known as the Seattle Spirit—made all the more intriguing because you have your work cut out for you when you try to find a Seattleite in the whole project.

Consider the Rainier Vista Women's Club. It took a war and a war-boom to produce anything like it. And it is about as typical of this wartime city as anything that has turned up.

Call the roll of its officers, and this is what you find: The president and her family came here within the past few months from Kansas; the vice president from Nebraska; the secretary from Oregon; the treasurer from Minnesota; the publicity chairman from North Dakota.

Before leaving Rainier Vista for a glimpse at some of Seattle's other housing developments, let's take a sample poll on the subject of civic affairs. Talk to Mrs. Loriece Sage, president; Mrs. Laura Armitage, treasurer, and Mrs. Madeline O'Brien, publicity chairman.

"Are you going to vote in the fall elections?"

"We'd like to," they chorus. "But you have to live in the city a year before you can vote. We'll have to wait until next year."

"I suppose," you ask, "that when the war-boom is over, all of you will leave Seattle and go back home?"

"No sir!" replies the youthful president, Mrs. Sage. "Seattle is my home now."

"Same here," says Mrs. O'Brien. "You couldn't get us back to North Dakota."

Mrs. Armitage thinks she and her family will return to Minnesota after the emergency. She thinks, however, that most Rainier Vistaites plan to stay right here. . . .

And on to one eye-opening subject after another: from the thriving shipyards in Bremerton across Puget Sound, turning out ships in record time for war . . . to Boeing's production-line output of airplanes . . . to the disappearance of those wondrous Northwest wild-blackberry pies (who would take time from war-profitable jobs to pick blackberries in forests and fields for bakeries and restaurants?) . . . to the still-colorful Pike Place Market, now noticeably more subdued without the interned Japanese farmers—and how seeing the tempting displays of farm produce you recall that the best peas bought in the New York markets this season came from Kent, a few miles from Seattle . . . to (sadly) the now-vanished cable cars that yielded to busses . . . to the city's rising birthrate—7,712 births in Seattle in 1941 compared with 4,919 in 1934 . . . to the feel of a newly blossoming metropolis.

Thus, my career as a working newspaperman closed on a dream assignment: Two weeks to explore wartime Seattle where and how I pleased, to interview anyone I chose, to write as I liked. This is how those stories looked in print in the Times.

Postwar years proved that people who came to see chose to stay—precisely as they did in 1909, the year of the Alaska-Yukon-Pacific Exposition.

And in the 1970s and 1980s, Seattle *did* take its place as one of the nation's mighty metropolises, expanding farther and farther into territory that in my time was way past the city limits and spawning satellite cities . . . its great water resources—four lakes within the city plus vast Lake Washington on its eastern shores, 1,800 miles of Pacific shoreline, easy access to the stunning San Juan Islands—all becoming vast recreational areas for sailing, yachting and other aquatic sports . . . its famed food and restaurants . . . its extensive theater, ballet and music gaining international renown . . . its industry, shipping and position in the world of finance—all expanding . . . its business districts blooming with skyscrapers that far outreach its once-tallest 42-story, 500-foot- high L. C. Smith Building.

Back in New York from our invigorating fling in my old city, returning to my research and writing in a pioneering field, I mulled it all over, recalling my dreams that never happened: of becoming city editor and one day managing editor of the *Seattle Times*.

And of my dream that *did* come true—being a newspaperman . . . and all the joy (if sometimes touched by a tear or two) that those newspaper years gave me . . . and the priceless experience—the priceless seasoning—that came with them.

But those days were over.

And now I realized that I no longer cared to have them back. However it was that I had been welcomed, encouraged, catapulted into a refreshingly different career, my days of longing for the life of a newspaperman were past.

I knew at last that I was happy to be in a creative new field of communications—public relations—to which I was making a substantial contribution and that it would be my way of life to the end.

Index